MINUTES
toward
NIGHT

MINUTES
toward
NIGHT

Quick Takes

William N. Gates

SUNSTONE
PRESS

SANTA FE

Sunstone books may be purchased for educational, business, or sales promotional use.
For information please write: Special Markets Department, Sunstone Press,
P.O. Box 2321, Santa Fe, New Mexico 87504-2321.

Book and Cover design › Vicki Ahl
Body typeface › Adobe Jenson Pro
Printed on acid-free paper
∞

Library of Congress Cataloging-in-Publication Data

Gates, William N., 1930-
[Poems. Selections]
Minutes toward night : poems / by W.N. Gates.
    pages cm
ISBN 978-0-86534-920-9 (softcover : alk. paper)
I. Title.
PS3607.A7888M56 2013
811'.6--dc23
                    2013006308

WWW.SUNSTONEPRESS.COM
SUNSTONE PRESS / POST OFFICE BOX 2321 / SANTA FE, NM 87504-2321 /USA
(505) 988-4418 / ORDERS ONLY (800) 243-5644 / FAX (505) 988-1025

FOREWORD

Like *River Riding Writing* and *In Words Dive,*
this book is composed of journal entries,
all of which were written within a limit of five minutes.
In that flash of time I would write as rapidly as possible,
ignoring punctuation and syntax, trusting in a coherence
of feeling or image. By transcribing this manuscript to print,
the impetus of handwriting is lost, but not,
I hope, the life that inspired it.

MINUTES toward NIGHT

"w" purses mouth in tight   "e" pushes mouth wide
to sides   "11" pulls tongue to sound roof of mouth like
clapper-bell   sound now: well   welling   wellness   will   wile
(longer)   wail (longer)   well   I'm well   as Katha
Pollit says   she could be a word   a word takes me over
like chord struck piano   I'm invaded by chord   it sends me
sounds me   ell   chord I found to   end piece
we embrace   it wraps me   I wrap it

December 31, 2003

      bedded in   crack of cliff   skeletal ruin   square
skull   skeletal litter   joints   eyes   they lived in
1000 years ago   fire only light short of stars and moon
firelight to fro   flash of faces   children   mates'
moments under covers   what pleasure in such shifting
fragrant light   burning down and down   embers
reveal sleeping heads and black hair   and closed eyes

February 4, 2004

      dilatory snow   dallying flake now and then   as
we pushed into voting place   slow line   formed into
snake coils to cram more people inside out of cold   but I
feel vitality   good humored   long line   waiting
edging forward   around to next coil   all Democrats
eager and not to be dissuaded by slow motion   enlivening
crowd cram   enlivened me at 4 am could not sleep for
thinking of faces   bodies all bundled up   one young
couple with baby and little girl

February 11, 2004

      smell of geranium   smell of boxwood   wet paths
sun shining weakly through last of rain   we walked down
knobby rumpled brick sidewalk toward bottom of
Georgetown   umbrellas dripping   backs of trousers
shoes soaking   sun and clouds drizzling
sky closes you in   compared to out here where it flings
away infinite in all directions   and always rhythmic earth
near and far   swelling up and down and up   higher and
higher   or like front of Jemez range   level chiaroscuro
of mesa-canyon-mesa   rhythmic dipping shadow-light-
shadow   gateways of rock and earth   opening inward
to labyrinth of tufa color

February 25, 2004

     our stretched figures   "and now release"   and on
into another figure twisting   stretching   holding
snow stretched far away   snow stitching as it was falling
falling all day long   stitch by stitch   white covers over
gradually disappearing trees   knitting trees to land   land
to hills to peaks   as we pulled ourselves toward calm
pulling our bodies   toward perfect obedience to her voice

March 10, 2004

     bad   bide   abide   bid   unbidden   bed
bead   bode   budding   body   of words
"sensuous to the nth degree" Suzanne Noguere   "how
body holds fast to pleasure"   Plath whatever else you say
Plath prepared a feast of words   as did Hopkins   Keats
Shakespeare   and I feast on her & their body of words
that's my communion biscuit & grape juice   my partaking
of their body of words   that nourish me   feed me
make me happy lifelong

March 24, 2004

     like someone expected to strut in a new mink coat or
tailored tuxedo   I put on sound of his piano   finding
fingers pressing harder into heavy keys   making sounds
too grand   deep velvety   for my chords   my tune
"just dreaming" cloaked in velvet & fur   but perhaps
could get used to such luxury of tone   heavy resistance of
keys   languor & reverberation of long   7   feet   of
piano

April 14, 2004

     Sunday it almost rained   but snowed   straight
down   just visible as sleet or snow   plumb down all day
Saturday cloudy again and we and urge to merge   urge to
splurge came over us   still traces of voluptuary oil   your
inner thighs   as my hand found time and again   and my
swelling pressed you to comply   to merge   me to surge
into you   surge   splurge   verge of splurge   when
I'm all lifted to top of fountain   before being dropped

May 30, 2004

     meadow   Big Tesuque Creek   step by step
closer to the clouds   plod   'sheer plod makes plough'
past vertical tones   bare aspen   bare still   ongoing
tones of water   full rush engulfing rocks   filling my ears
& brain   tree tones straight as rain   tones curved
bent bow   low   tired of freeways & flyways   crash of
falls   heavy plunging   hollows out a pool
 pool beyond pool

May 31, 2004

     so ice cold my bones ached dipping hand in power
source   pool backed up behind great wrecked fir   deep
still room gold   brown   shifting shadows   high up
aspen   water poured out sideways   behind pour   lines
of ripple   sinuous back & forth wavering   staying
precise moving parallels   up tapering stump strict parallels
graved   gray wood   grain flowed upward   each
swerve   lines all stayed exact parallels   all up pinnacle
ruined cathedral   trembled strands   webs   old nets

June 1, 2004

   "how with this rage shall beauty hold a plea"   how
with this rush shall anything be kept   myself walking
along a hall along a street   intent on getting somewhere
once in a while stopped by a mass of azalea   but mostly
just intent on pursuit of something – a train   an exhibit
an errand   a "walk" over so familiar territory I hardly
notice   if it weren't for these books what would I
remember?   what would I keep?   doubtless something
but most would be gone as if it never happened

June 7, 2004

   that cloud stays with me   overshadowing Baldy
darkening all its slopes & steeps   sunlit edges   bright
around gray interior   it slowly   grand   remote
solid-nebulous   thick   vapor   drafty   raft
shifting   round   raft   cloud   so single   shape
ship   slowly plying   north   stays with me   in that
moment of our perching   high over   deep swooping
valley   sound of swollen creek   and shifting swaying
of spruce

June 9, 2004

    Old Shipyard you named it   not a trace of snow on
this slope   cool   clouds   creek still roaring   down
from lake   tall pole still   still held   steadied by young
tree   tall   gray   spare   bitten   another
singular   not propped or steadied   to my push it
wobbled   unsteady in its socket   not long for
perpendicular   but for the time being   pointing to high
clouds   nicked   gnawed   scarred by lightning   fire
and weather   14 feet of rugged silvery mast   you caught
yourself saying   better get out the silver polish   this
your favorite place   on your favorite trail

June 14, 2004

    as held in 2 cupped hands   water spilling
refilling   pooled but not still   cupped stone & gravel
gold and brown   held me quiet   surrounded by roar
held by cupped restless pool   islands of green lambency
tall upshoots of magenta blossoms   brilliant green
hellebore   pileup of sticks   wrecks   roots   held
water   and held me

July 5, 2004

      at Bill Stewart's   way back up Arroyo Pequeño in
Tesuque hills   I as I talked to young Chandler from Atlanta
who'd flown in for Janie's 80th Yankee Doodle Dandy
birthday   I watched children clamber up hill behind B's
house all the way to sunlit top   where they found steel
stakes to duel with   this a very different gathering
      Janie looked so pretty   80 and so pretty
Chandler told me of J   what she'd been in his life   how
she'd taken him in   backed him up at critical time   and
I kept watching kids dueling   down steep slope   after
sunset   in afterlight of those hills   in cool dry air

July 19, 2004

      over and over in my head that song   but _that_ version
over & over   *Begin the Beguine*   Artie Shaw's   Ann
Little heard it over & over   crossing ocean before war
played it over & over again   again the Beguine   what
hooks it to me now?   what sticks it in my round & round
memory   turntable   that little 10" hard black disc
they (we) played it till it was all scratches   I grew up with
it in the '40s   danced it   hummed it   his words lost
what were they   no one knew   but everyone knew that
melodious mellow   melancholic   melanzane   melony
melting   melody

July 29, 2004

      cling   clung   cloud   climb   clouds
collide   as I watch   change slow colliding   join
swell   transforming   so slowly   softly   vaporous
various grays to white   so swiftly in absence of watching
eyes return   find them all transformed   eyes lower to
see their shadows overwhelming   mountains   I sat
silent   unmoving   unwriting   undrawing   while
you read   and on way descending   my thoughts went
down: maybe I wasn't good for you   no fun   no talk
not a companion   but these down thoughts were later
dispelled by you   my mind like a mass of changeable
cloud

July 30, 2004

    High Meadow, Big Tesuque   sun under cloud
monkshood ultramarine springs to view   blue dark &deep
seems to float against greens   this spring-fed garden of
monk's ultra   hot yellow daisies (helenium)   Indian
paintbrush   hare-bells   tall grasses   white   lacy
delicate places   tensile aspen   minuscule stream
trickling water walk   moss   plants   blossoms
ultramarine dabs   twinkling yellows & whites
quivering shadows

August 11, 2004

    1946-47   *Blue Moon*   band played
casino dance   Salters Point   couples pressed close
hands clasped   swayed side to side   Frankenstein style
Dave Perry said "Did you dance with Schlop? Do you like
Schlop?"   yes she was cute   tied up with that name that
she spoke in a slur to soften it   Schlop or Schlap from St.
Louis   pretty with dark hair   blue eyes   "Blue
Moooon …"   small delicate Sylvia Schlop   no one else
do I remember   I told her she was best-looking girl there
and she said "so are you"   she was being sweet   I
didn't believe it   but I learned better dancing   by
and   by

August 19, 2004

    despite delicate rippling of Bach   his insistent beat
and   persistent pattern pattering   one's ears take in
extraneous noise   loud motors out on street   thunder of
breaking storm   coughs   flapping of paper   feet
shuffling up balcony   then ears return to be taken   by
those dancey sounds rippling out of keyboard   Fr. Suite #6
(and I recall picking out some of it at 22-21)   this child
was playing softly & precisely   then finally after too-long
program doors opened to rain   and we with no umbrella

August 25, 2004

       engrave   grave   grove   enclose   enclosing
me   path overweeded   trail   desuetude   blocked
deadfallen   many athwart   had to skirt or clamber over
gates closed   nature wards   protects   this place
but I made it through one more time   stood below
among   enclosed grove   up   tops   swayed   far
up tops swayed   swell of wind   roared   dwindled to
silk   I said I can't go back to what I was   not 10 years
ago   not 5   no more can these   that seemed immortal

August 22, 2004

       as we ate watched   fat chipmunks   each on its
perch   stuffing selves with your crusts   afterward
we followed stumbly desultory devious path around & in &
out   up & down   around lake to its source   followed
right to the kiss that met us then close by waterfalls   juicy
kiss a festival kiss to commemorate   our close clasping at a
tree   while hail thrashed ground & trees all around   in
that   steaming   chilled air of high July

August 26, 2004

rain   that soaked wilderness we walked in   rain
that soaked red punk-loaded hulks   that brought forth
gentians' peerless blue-power   was in the making   was
impending   was looming   immense to our eyes as we
topped crest of canyon and looked toward Taos   across
huge black crack of gorge   northward   sweeping
now all being engulfed by immense rainstorm
white-cracked by lightning   storm-blue   gentian-blue
and was even now invading & blurring   high peaks
surely this would drench us   we were there   we saw it
I'm here to tell you.

August 30, 2004

as I sat across gun'ls of an old broken barque   on its
cargo of rust rot riches   I thought I'd come to more ease
from that moment downtown   road rage at jeering fool that
offended me   and realized that wheel-club would make a
killing club (but it could be taken from me etc.)   chain of
troubles occupied me as I climbed trail   and weakened me
and I saw that rage weakens   rage blinds   rage doesn't
work

August 30, 2004

     What finally perked me up   set me right with the
world   was that young mother of 4   down in the parking
lot   her easy humorous good looks   as she spread her
child's wet shorts on rear windshield wiper   turned to me
with a big smile   and seeing my smile said "he wasn't here
even half an hour before he fell in"   wet pants hung from
stuck-out wiper: a family flag

September 6, 2004

     hymn   hum home   whom   is it   hymn sing
school chapel   "God of our faaa …"   stuck in memory
what's next   "… thers whose almighty hand …"   what
next   more junk   bits   fragments   stuck   like
"see the USA in a Chevrolet"   but oh how they stick
"how the body holds fast to …" one word will cue another
piece of something   trash or gold   Janie Farrar recalled
our deep window sills in Arroyo Hondo   she and Sarah
would play in them   they were like alcoves   or rooms
our deep-set adobe window-reveals

October 7, 2004

     even no sun I sensed their luminous presence   high
above   as I labored up trail (so much longer than I'd
thought and I at rope end of fatigue)   somber dark   wet
from great rain day before   I seem to trudge in darkness
heavy fatigue   but   I felt their radiant airy presence
each delicate mobile leaf   ready to sway   to wave   to
shimmer   as one in darkness of audience looks toward
brightly lit dancers on stage

October 11, 2004

     yellow fire   bursts out of dark country   could be
magma   lava   spurts across cooling dark-moving flow
except this land stopped   and stayed put now millions ago
and seeming flames are cool   shimmering   patches in
dark evergreen forests   where we climb trail that holds us
steadies us   upward past one ponderosa   and   another
in this realm of rich-robed pines   ahead to westward we see
distant gray rock peaking up   skimmed with snow

November 8, 2004

aspen?   pine?   no telling now   bark stripped
smooth   gray   bare   young thing   sapling   now
in-   through-   after-death assuming its final figure
its final asana   two long twigs   curling down and
around to meet   all other twigs like them in final
down-curl   its stem rising in slight twists and bends   it
stands solitary   I noticed as we talked   I looked at it
again   I looked at it   thinking   "well …" then at last
saying   "I guess I've got to draw that"

November 8, 2004

white?   pink?   no telling now   but it was to-
the-floor   but I see her smile   Puffin at 14   she stood in
front of me   where I skulked at edge of dance floor
she smiled   what smile?   timid   bold   scared
adventurous   determined to get me to dance with her
"Billy?" she said to me   her gauche   unhappy
un-danceable cousin   never'd been dancing before   not
for real   "Billy?"   her sweet eager   not bold   but
bold enough   and so   we danced

November 12, 2004

     sidestepping those furies   climbing beyond
bitterness   we came upon a happy day   with bright new
snow mountains gleaming far ahead   past shorn aspen with
their own sunlit radiance   past columns of evergreen
stepping upward on even gradient   gradually rising trail
patches still dark mud from melted snow
     dry crinkled aspen   leaves on top   we walked
vigorously   gained our meadow in an hour + 10   our
day mellowed onward from that walk

November 18, 2004

     as I climbed I began to see them   for the first time
saw them: one   then another   and another
scattered over ground   flakes of matte color   ocher
mustard   pink   burnt sienna   no shiny like obsidian
no gleamy like quartz   but chips of matte   like chalk
or pastel   they seized my senses   I picked one up
then another   chips of a crumbling sandstone or
sedimentary matrix   everywhere I looked   I loved those
matte tints   I took samples   turned in sunlight   tiny
sparks   as of farthest remote stars

November 18, 2004

       I hug them to myself   fastened to them   as by
pieces of time   linkage   chronos   cronies   was that when
Ann said that   and that was a year before we put the house on
the market   when we stayed at Lennie's house
Ann asked "Why do you want to go back to Santa Fe?"
knowing in her heart she detested idea   would never go
back unless forced   year later (at another friend's house)
we agreed to sell house   <u>agreed</u>   I in full accord –
because how could I or we rattle around in it alone or 2?
we   I   knew we could not keep it if we didn't live in it
besides from Phila   where I was bonded by then   Santa
Fe seemed paltry   poor   no place to live   this to
answer my inner howl of nostalgia   why did I leave it
why did I sell it?

November 26, 2004

    I was bent on being cool to protect myself from
mockery   as when Larry sent his girlfriend to sit on my lap
I knew they were watching   laughing   behind me
I worked to be cool   unperturbed   as she sat on me with her
blond braids & bucktoothed smile (she was just as
speechless as I – only doing what he told her)   I clamped
my pipe in my mouth   that had a bowl carved in a skull
and on my head was black Nazi cunt cap Uncle Geof sent me
from Europe   when I think what an odd boy I must have
seemed   I smile   perfecting my composure (with a
smokeless pipe and a Nazi cunt cap)   summer of VJ
1945   "Now if you want to hear some boogie then I know
the place …"

December 13, 2004

    first you had that sexy dream (and the dream within the
dream: recipe for warm dream salad)   then we
woke   when you came back to bed you were naked
and on we went from there   into such delights   that
evening you pushed back table and we danced (practice) on
good wood floor   Diana Krall moved us along and I learned
your steps   (country & western next night at party
we'd practiced for   no good   jump   bounce &
heehaw music)

March 7, 2005

      always: where to dive in   arrow-pointing hands
where   here   long honk from river   prolonged train-
wail of happy jazz   Vieux Carre   houses no more than 2
stories   West Indian colors   lacy iron veils over
balconies   and flowers and greens tumbling   and that
corner   Ursulines & Chartres   yellow geranium leaf
recalls   ocher house with blue-gray shutters
Beauregard – Keyes   its stepped-up portico   wide
fanlight   tall door   tall windows   with traced
transoms

March 9, 2005

      toothless old black man   in white waiter-jacket
knitted wool cap   brought breakfast tray: fresh o.j.
café au lait   sumptuous biscuits   in a basket
wrapped in napkin kept hot by a hot tile in bottom   and did I
butter them? and jam them with homemade strawberry?
"I got a right to sing the blues …"   as we walked along
near r.r. tracks & river (morning)   passed café & small
band playing   and   man who sang "I got a right to sing
the blues …"   but not gloomy blues   a lifting blues
and it was morning

March 10, 2005

      uncoiling dark from newel   sinuous   rising
handling   rippled banister   it swings   up around out of
sight   describing flight of steps   that turn fan-wise so
close & tight at axis   no foot can follow   up we go (or
down we carefully step)   to 2nd floor   to left   hall
ushers toward door embroidered by windows each side
and over top   to right through another door   down steps
to balcony   (not gallery – not wide enough)   connecting
rooms   we enter   another tall narrow double door
and room   of white painted brick encloses   high ceiling
and bed with a coronal fall & spread

March 10, 2005

      you better believe it   you better <u>believe</u>   (GI
faces rise to mind)   you better believe   (because if you
don't, look out)   it was cold   windy   up on levee
we walked   watching huge ships   approach bridge
(would they clear it)   river narrowed   bulling along at 7
knots   to right we looked down   you better <u>believe</u>
down on precarious city   still there   under threat of
hurricane or rampaging sea   or Mississippi power
or yellow fever   city on edge of calamity

March 11, 2005

      dream   our seats in theater were behind one another
in Row I   and rows   went not across   but up &
down-slope   then you went off   I saw by my watch
there was lots of time   before show   so I could go back
to house to get something I needed   outside it was dark
streets obscure   which was right?   I took one that led
me upward   no sidewalk   walls right to edge   so I
clung close to wall   then I saw it was wrong st.   where
to go?   then around corner came streetcar   all brightly
lit   incandescent streetcar   missed me   because I
stuck close to wall   (and you dreamt you lost me)
(while I was losing myself)

March 16, 2005

      headless ghosts   occupy our white deck chairs
chair arms overlapped by theirs   their round knees curving
down   to great skirts that hide their feet
conversation languid   white on white   hovered over by
white bear-paws   of trees drooping humbled   gradually
in time   puffs of air   nudge wads off them   they
spring and nod in release   and air disperses wads in white
mist   that trails and twists away

July 21, 2005

    stretchability   Tanya seated   tucked one foot
with active big toe into her crotch   extended other foot out
to side   raised naked arms straight over head and bent
far over to one side   until her clasped fingers rested on that
distant active big toe   she   her yoga   brings me to a
kind of peace   "almost peace"   beyond her beauty &
woman power   because aware of one's own reverence
reverent positions   reaching more and more

August 30, 2005

    from my corner of earth   my corner of womanhood
from where I nestled between your hips   between your
thighs   I could look up   get a foreshortened view of
your landscape   and it became as long & broad as the
whole earth   shaded and lightened as the other
mesa of your rib cage   peaks of your breasts   distant
Pedernal of your chin from underneath   and my hands
reaching up along your womanly earth   found your skin
voluptuously sleek and rich

September 1, 2005

       fade   toward the shade   fade   raid   invade
made   got it made   in the shade   Korea   see green
men   their green clothes   new dull green   old washed
& washed   until nearly white   men in green   I've-
you've-we've got it made   and fade   toward the shade
my fantasy factory   mixing lust and dream   forever
mixing concrete or cement sludge   making visions   sex
fantasies   fancies   fanciful brain breeding   what out
of dead land   not lilacs   faded men in green caps
got it made in the shade

October 6, 2005

       as icy white vapors   writhe   wither   twist
shred   vanish into blue   wind that blows them sets up a
great shimmer in the aspen slope   and it spreads from
yellow to red to green   as I climb (and return down again)
my eyes keep searching high-up   tatters of yellow   to
see dark blue piercing through   spearing   tattering
yellow   dark & intense   I keep looking for it   and
blue notes of *Stormy Weather*   I try over & over in mind
it's blues   perfect blue notes & chords   I sound it over
& over

October 10, 2005

    smell of yesterday's   day before's   fallen
blackening   covering year before's   now and then
faintest   most fleeting scent of shriveling   as we made
our way up along Wilderness fence   and in a luminous
pattern   now's   falling   settling on ground
some places so numerous   reds   yellows   they gave
light   luminous spotting against black   formers and
latters   against black micaceous earth

October 17, 2005

    still intact   delicate   small   gray   bare of
bark (something stopped it early in life)   all its
down-curling boughs   still as if describing big circles
bigger than they can compass   this fine little sapling dry of
sap   I take 4 different angles   and draw   to try to
keep a record of it   we saw it last November   and
wondered would it still be there   I think about it when
I'm not there   now behold   still there   intact

October 26, 2005

explore tenses   would   will   all enclosed in
was   and have been   what shock   (the time would
come)   what jolt to them to know   if they could have
foreseen how short their time would be in that place
which in time's slow exploding   would be acceptable
even right to them   as they set forth   and left this house
on their separate ways   not even if they only knew
a family any more   unforeseeable   but in time they
would acquiesce   inevitable in its working out   but back
then hardly thinkable   unthinkable

November 5, 2005

like stage back wall   that tall rock   pinks
ochers   beige   all light   all reflecting   against
which they bowed   this way & that   dancers you said
black against light   all trees became figures   black
passersby   or   dancers   or yoga practicers   black
against that tremendous glow   which also touched
surface of water   in pools of pink or beige   sun had
already set behind ridge at 1 pm   all we walked   all
amid the faint nostalgic scent of decaying leaves

November 5, 2005

      it is and is and is   rock   tall   down-carved and
cracked   gargoyled   they are   and were   and have
been   leaves   delicate shriveled paper   some cut
round   some narrow pointed   most recent (latters) bright
enough to cast light upward   (formers) befores & befores
faded pale tan or ocher   how they track and shush
underfoot   how they smell   some thick matted behind
stream rock   gathered waiting   to sink or to flow
onward

November 23, 2005

      so   when we collided   when we exploded   in
our fusion   in our melting   molten   you gave me not
only yourself   but myself   another life and self I never
dreamed I had   and in our furnace and molten mating   I
gave you myself and your self too   and you've thrived
upon it ever since   thrived   thriven   thrive
live   chive   lived   rive
riven   both riven   torn wide open
to receive   each other's gift

February 23, 2006

"Matisse is dead"   how untouched most were by
Nov. 3 1954 (now a date to reverberate)   filled up full as we
were   by subways   trains to catch   consumed by
squalid hotel rooms   by medieval art and stained glass of
Sainte Chapelle   plans for Italy and Christmas back home
and going back to school   to be a writer   now with a
lifetime growing into seeing the great artist and his works
now it seems "November 3, 1954"   and where was I?   I
was there in France   being pulled along   sucked along
into future glories   or miseries

February 24, 2006

Gloria   sic transit   sic pouf   Gloria who?
Jones   tall   blond   short shingle bob (1954)   rather
long face   full lips   big smile   I see her in long gray
coat she went out in   Paris ocean-liner romance that
seemed to evaporate when our feet came to streets   one
week   one step from glory to humiliation   I danced one
night with her (first class she was) on floor of glass with
lights glowing underfoot   spent a week glorifying her
then our next & last meeting   Paris   we walked
night by Seine   and hardly spoke a word to each other back
to her hotel   bye   nice to see you etc

February 27, 2006

        despair   disrepair   spare   scant   scarce
scared   screwed   that dream   bad out of age old
never quite forgotten   fear of being betrayed & abandoned
as you said common   you have dreams of losing me in
crowds   I dreamed of someone else taking you over   of
you sliding away to another   and I said I shouted "I'm mad
sick mad"   had to rise out of dejection of dream   you
helped me   believe?   I believe you   mountain of
evidence for belief   no evidence for disbelief   but it just
came out of old sewer pit   childhood

March 10, 2006

        "that's an easy one" she said   stretching   flexing
herself into figure to mirror picture on cover Yoga mag
easy   easy   and then she stretched up both elbows up &
over her head   reached both hands back   tipped her
head back & back   both hands back & back to take hold of
foot raised up behind her   ah   ah   as she might say
correcting you   divinity I said   ah   ooh   yes
Tanya goddess   would there be room for a man in her life
if he got down on all fours   agreeable to occasional
fondling   watering   feeding   maybe those creatures
those pets are really all her other admirers   former

April 14, 2006

      when I was 16 - 17   I saw picture   little
European waif   a war waif with great big dark eyes staring
out at me   and that pushed me toward foreign service as a
way to take care of her and others like her   she pulled me
then later pull petered out   I went to D.C. to talk to people
to interview   then-Democrat State Dept   loyalty oaths
stopped me   and other discouraging things   then came
Republican State Dept   I turned away altogether   saw
myself as romantic   naïve   but why State Dept with all
its protocol & claptrap? why not UNRRA   or a relief
organization that would have put me face to face with that
waif and so many others?

April 14, 2006

      instead of being harnessed & put to work   directly
to the point   pull crumbled dissolved into air   in
dementia of youth: spasms of desire   of horseplay   of
gaiety   of aimless energy   amid that I felt a push of
idealism no less strong or futile than World Federalism &
those who solemn & holy adopted it (I scorned them) but that
I kept to myself   I must have seemed a right ninny to them
but was really only being jerked around (jerked off) by the
demon of youth   in aimless leaps & kicks

May 17, 2006

     (back from Florence) Donatello   Mary Magdalene
hung   hanks   ropes   tatters of her wavy hair that
covered her down to her knees   tattered   ragged as an
ancient hulk of wood in a forest   she seemed to falter
forward   one foot molding itself to stone   another foot
drawn back & knee bent as it paused in mid-step   her
hands raised   fingers not quite touching   in prayer?
her head tilted to one side   shadows gathered under
hollows of cheeks   and caves of eyes   her neck eaten
away almost to bone   her bare arms not decayed but thin
and muscular as rope   yes Magdalene   but beyond
confines of that myth   imploring   a survivor of Dachau
beseeching

May 31, 2006

     gospel song we sang when we were training for war:
"I'm gonna lay down my sword and shield down by the
riverside   ain't gonna study war no more"   stone
bone   crone   Mary Mag. as a crone   drone   lone
crone   sewn   sown   forlorn   why we men learn
only when we're old   too old to study war no more   and
not make war   sown   words on stone   falling on
stone   blown   words   her long shaggy hair   her
two teeth jut up in her lower jaw

June 12, 2006

     what was I playing   Dark Blue   low rolling bass
top trill   when you came weaving   undulating   were
going to take a bath   but were magnetized by my piano
and came swaying   undulating   (reminds me   your
undulating song   that sometimes sounds from you out of
nowhere   as if you were touched by such sensual memory
it went all through you and provoked that voluptuous
undulating song)

June 29, 2006

      fondle   dandle   kindle   kind   find   fond
fend   friend   random fondle   draw them through my
fingers   long satin-smooth green ribbons   of lavish wild
flourishing   beside tiny stream   if they could know how
I love them   even though I sit on them & crush them
(but I don't eat them)   just so   fondling   as I would
Helen's bunch of hair   that plump round bundle of silver &
black   stroke grasses & lift each blossom to study
behind black dart a yellow collar defined by red scalloped
collar

June 29, 2006

      shooting star   monkshood   geranium
Hopkins calls: "Each mortal thing   Deals out that being
indoors each one dwells"   but myself   to speak and
spell   my original raw singular self   to be what I do
"what I do is me   for that I came"   what's left of a
singular self   after being divided   diverted
sidestreamed   swamped & driven underground   if only I
could have kept all   I did keep something   it comes out
now here & there   but

July 17, 2006

    glowing paintbrush amid grosser forms of life like
occasional misshapen tree that rises into trident forks   or
like Van Gogh's pollarded trees   chopped & coarse
peasant faces   hands   remember us teens at Groton
coarse & lumpish   honks & jeers   blares of laughter
"variously sprouting"   and the one delicate beautiful one in
our midst who drew our admiration (secret) desire & love
my eyes are drawn to wildflowers   stones   relics of
wood on ground   my eyes in admiration and desire

July 24, 2006

    rapid   but luminous   pointing out rhythms
shimmering   I call back   recall   scraps   phrases
of Partita #5   as he played   comparing his tempo   his
skill with my old set of Paul Badura-Skoda from 1950-51
that now in memory sounds bit clunky   halting compared
to this   buoyant   luminous   light   fluttering
but with persistent beat   sometimes light   sometimes
sharply percussive   so hard to write of music   non-
technically   notes   keys   sharps   etc   but it
gave us a lift   a big lift to go that Sat. afternoon and hear
that Bach

July 27, 2006

    I pull away shriveled bark   bronze with black
markings   shields   a shield to admire and place   pull
away dried rags of clothing   to bare smooth round inner
tree   to find tones of brown and gray   I am more true to
these   than to dreams of glory   of women   of Tanya
in all her splendor   because seeming to dwell on one I
switch to another woman and even to a form I conjure up
fickle I go on and on   until I have to laugh at my silliness
enduring   ephemeral   licks

August 10, 2006

    high   higher   so high   so close to clouds
sometimes above   sometimes in them   feel nuzzling of
their cold mist   yesterday up boundary trail   at meadow
on quartzy promontory   all sparkling mica & quartz
clouds built up a tower above me   saw them grow &
expand as I watched   their edges round & sharp & tense
against deepest darkest blue   uplook as with tallest
skyscraper   or cliff thousands of feet perpendicular
then downlooking   into deeper darker farther reaches
thundering dark blue   powerhouse of clouds

October 5, 2006

      tide of sleep rolls you over on back   sprawled   in
dark your imaginable curves & mounds   knees   feet
and up and over mons   under covers but prominent
then outgoing tide rolls you up on side where my hand once
again finds your hip and above   and below   carved
curved   smoothed by waves   eons of waves & tides
to a malleable strokeable stone   where my hand finds
pleasure   and finally peace   though it now & then roams
down slope to cove and up bluff of ribcage   a sort of
predictable haven

October 25, 2006

      enduring   ephemeral   licks   "yet knowing
how way leads on to way"   one note   one word   one
letter's change brings change   of mood   yesterday on
piano   one note of chord   change of color   Frost
"Woodpile"   he found a treasure in woods (as I found
treasure on Rowe Mesa) someone's hoard   a cord of maple
all cut split & stacked   4 x 4 x 8   forgotten?   no
never forgotten   but lost   the gatherer   the cutter left
it   meant to return & take   but when he got home
something happened   one thing came up   and another
and time passed   and when he returned to take his treasure
he could not find his way back to it

November 13, 2006

     and that song   sparked by the notes of a moment
goes on & on through a million more moments   goes
tootling & noodling on   until it's like rotting withering
flowers   that you can't throw out   it's stuck
moments am are is was were   am are is was were   they
follow or flow not to the beat of minutes   but expandable
shorts or longs   long am's   long is's   short was's
waste was

November 16, 2006

dream:
     our tour guide (Fr.) took us down hill   in his strange
dragging contrivance   industrial wasteland   to his
special art studio   sculptor made objects of metal   we
were urged to admire & buy   then back we went dragging
uphill   and took huge elevator   Helen nowhere in sight
a Fr. woman foundering   I helped her to seat   *"Mais ou
sont les autres qui etaient avec nous?"* I said   she didn't
know   my femme   her mari   then I broke into Sp.
"como de constumbre" I said   she smiled and said
"olé olé"   then I woke up   and that moment was gone
but I've brought it back   some piece of it

November 24, 2006

    tawny   tan   ocher   beige   russet   various
intricacies   once and only uprising   from one rainy spell
conjured them up out of stony gritty soil   look at them
sun-caught   brilliant   pale   dry   dying   drying
billowing under us as we lie back   fragrant   faint
pungence of their drying   what a glorious mortality
grama lofting above rest with their curled comma heads stiff
waving   silky brushy thing   something   become all
white   long bristles and seeds   rusty russet clouds of
intricate branching   and towering over all   black piñons
dead of beetle devouring   shorn and stark

December 6, 2006

    peer   poire   compare   beyond compare
pure   pear   into my dry mouth   thirsting   knife
point   pierced   drew narrow slice   out of and into me
mouth far corners   crannies   infused   cool   sweet
nectar   juicy   in me   such flood of marvelous merest
fruit   that thin wedge enraptured   rippled all through
dry tongue and cheeks and teeth   mere peerless pear
could not believe would give me so much

January 4, 2007

    5 o'clock   final lookback through snowy trees
parting retrospect before twilight   dusk   dark   its red
round beam   catches   pastel in hall   just that picture
Grand Canyon abstracted   and sets it afire   never such
color   never such glow   composed of grainy strokes of
golden ocher chalk   purple chalk   reds   yellows
see even sandy grit of paper   last review of sun gives me
the picture as never seen before   down it goes   horizon
closes it off   trees blacken before enormous red glow of
twilight   picture dims & dulls   red glow is all in sky
spreading   dilating over west   while moon   full
moon rising   east

January 30, 2007

    studied uprising fibers gray precise parallels
where they flowed   curved & twisted   the tree upward
branching telling   crying its story to the blurred sun   old
stripped juniper top of Frey trail   "what I do is me   for
that I came"   and why or where no matter   I tell my tale
as I came down into canyon   wondered: what does Peaslee
think of his life   has it been a success? I thought and I said
my life has been successful   I triumphed over all those
burdens & impediments that dogged me & dragged me down

March 19, 2007

dreams 2

   I'd come back from a long journey on a ship to
retrieve things left behind (not taken not packed) and inside
large compartment under bunk I found pieces of clothing
pieces of Chinese brocade old Chinese embroidered purse
from childhood from Da 2 prs loafers which I tossed
into wastebasket things no longer needed left behind
I could let them go to go on into future
   I was looking for a church and I went in to a
church not pews in long rows but carved painted
benches here & there the preacher was a woman in her
pulpit youngish she smiled and laughed as she talked
laughing she drew us in I went in to listen

April 23, 2007

   her nose aquiline sharp delicate narrow
as always her face still striking but ragged haggard
teeth showing more falsity hair colored blond
voice halting struggling for word so you wait in
suspense for what word is she groping for ?
then it comes then another struggle he used to finish
her sentences now released from his oppression how
will she live free?

April 26, 2007

     his hands rippled up & down the keyboard   gliding
glissando   Liberace-style   he smoked a pipe all the
while   smoke poured out of pipe like a smokestack   and
he began to sing in falsetto   a yowling accompaniment
what a dream   maybe I heard howl of dog or coyote in my
sleep   pipe-smoking & "tickling the ivories" as they used
to say   he had a moustache and his pipe was gushing
smoke
     and here I am   drinking coffee   taste   smell
bring back life before Helen   I drank it and smoked like a
smokestack for years

May 3, 2007

by Tesuque Cr.
     inner-outer   inside sounds   outside sounds
inside: "Just Dreaming"   final chords   heard clear
and I try them
     outside: swollen tumbling water   such a glut and
glunk   further up: chickadee   jay   hermit thrush
so this thin skull separates them   and they are heard
simultaneously
     ceaseless   luscious   rush
     & chords

May 7, 2007

      words   chords   word   chord   now at
distance of time & space   I still see water   but can
hardly hear it   chords still resonate   Sat. noon in MRI
tunnel   close metal cave I lay in   such noise attacked
me   I couldn't think or remember   my brain   my ears
into brain   assaulted   no memory   no inner sound
could compete   snuffed out by such racket   measured
electronic racket   dahda dahda dahda   d-d-d-d-d
whang whang whang   as to strip away all sense   could
only endure until it quit

May 7, 2007

      another chord to be added   just a half-tone change
b to b-flat   and final 6th   peace   tranquility
solved   plashing water   up from my perch a low
cascade   chopped & battered water churning up bubbles
foam that vanished in passing   by the time it reached my
position it funneled into a smooth tongue that raced through a
breach and divided left and right   left doubling back
hairpin twist   right straight on   shapes & sounds of
water

May 24, 2007

      by finesse of placed steps   creeping   careful
straddling   climbing   footing downward   I was able to
push up farther than before   in recent times   and so
found a piece of what I'd lost   a piece of 1980   that
rocky slot and white cataract   pounding down through
despite huge timbers athwart it burst through   intent
bent   bound   bounding   down its well-carved way
I was able to recover something – and a model of that
churning bubble pool that healed me when I was 50
pleased and delighted

May 28, 2007

confuse   but a certain wandering way   only path
through wilderness   my brain   my stream of awakeness
at 3 in dark of night   succession of music   succeeding
songs   "Someone to watch over me"   to music of
wedding   Sept.   Golden Gate Park   &   trumpet
rising high into cold stream of fog   to "Gonna take
a sen ti mental journey"   languid lullaby summer 1945
confusing but wayward   onward   as now I watch
second hand   nudging onward mincing time into small
measure   can't see that in dark   then at last asleep
when it comes   what brings it   how I enter it   what
image   what dream   lost

May 29, 2007

     only path through wilderness of brain   wayward
onward   memories pouring in   New Mexico (old times
1956) was a powerful place   enchanted I was by the very
air and light   summer   7 pm   late relenting sun cast
long shadows   clouds shreds very white   light &
shadow of clouds   air dry   crisp   winey
embracing   its presence   my skin told me this was
enchantment   heaven after crushing sticky heat of East
unbearable to almost unbearable skin delight of air   New
Mexico exerted a pull like nothing else   even women
I had to live here in its embrace

June 28, 2007

     blossom   cloud   watch   we 2   H & I   up
high   we separately watched   perched ½ mile apart
watched same big cloud blossom   its top edges taut
sharp   bulging up
     she could not see blue & gray lower depths of it which
I saw   Baldy lifted it   mountains pushed it up
     towering so high   at last it began to soften   dissolve
drift   smear southward   others began to tower up

July 23, 2007

       ooze   ruse   choose   muse   maze   amaze
I dreamed I held a baby months-old   but it talked   we
talked   he talked   given charge of baby by someone
I was holding him up   his head wobbled unsteady   but
he talked to me   we talked   H. thinks advent of a new
project for me   in words   this newborn   what?   I
keep thinking   gazing on my child portrait in its glowing
new frame   maybe that's the new project   why did it
take me so long to get a new frame for that child?

July 26, 2007

       spritz   or trickle   or leak   of music   always
in mind   forest cold soaking wet   dark   dank
smelling   evergreens poked up toward sullen sky   I
pushed upward   seemed heavier going   I labored
hips hurt   back hurt   would I get up top overlook
doubtful   earth & path soaked   raddled   troweled by
rain   eyes fastened on footing ground   rain had
streamed down pushing clots of needles   I rested by
wilderness gate   went on climbing   forest dreary in
imminent rain   rain impending

July 30, 2007

     final   finial   foam   refining   finito   finite
finish   finish waves' overlapping   unrolling
(mats or carpets)   farthest extent   smoothing   see
them coming   oncoming   "in sequent toil"
remembering Point Reyes lighthouse high-placed on
promontory   gave long views of coast north and south and
out to sea   and we overlooked white waves far below
rolling   successive   obsessive   smoothing
munching on that soft hilly rolling coast   until lost to sight
under white mist of wave spray

August 22, 2007

     back from Alaska   massive growl   engines
revving up at 6 am   no sleep after   we were moving
engines roaring higher and higher   from stern amid deep
roar & grind & howl   saw wake curving away   sinuous
pathway froth   staring at churned up water   froth
bubbles   bobulating   those sunny days   gave faroff
glimmer of dreamy snows just separating from pale horizon
great jags & peaks faint in distance   closer saw gazed
snow dapples   forms of snow sprawled over mountains

August 22, 2007

      swoop up sheer up from level sea   mountains up tall
thousands higher than Sangre de Cristo abrupt up from water
dark backs dappled pied with snow-forms   pinto
mountains I wanted to draw but didn't (I did draw glaciers)
and down from those wild heights tumbled streams
cascades   one on top of another   white water down to
salt water   their green pale viridian influenced sea to turn
sea green icy green palest viridian   my eyes drawn to
green sheen viridian waves   rolling away from cut-water
ship

August 27, 2007

      floating lights   ice sculpted   licked   melted
down to little craft   bird shapes   drifting by on icy green
water   remnants of bergs   calves of glacier
thunderclaps after fall of ice   crash   crack   boom
off those ramparts white pinnacles turrets that ice comes to in
its flow slow towards sea   from ancestral everwhite
mountain turrets   ice mass arrives at water   starts to
divide vertical into towers that crumble   crash

September 3, 2007

      bear cubs romped   rollicking ran   chased each
other   one went off into water   splash   other ran
stopped   rounded on its sibling and charged   they rose
up to each other   cuffed   wrestled   jaws opened to
bite   long jaws   they did it over & over again   like
me and Geof as kids in pool   never seemed never to tire of
it   rollicking gait   both hind legs flying up behind
all of us humans in kayaks & inflatable launch watched in
awed silence in delight

September 20, 2007

      behind closed eyes   see gentian   blue stars
some pale as sky   some deep as cobalt   even
sapphire   goblet   goblin   stars   and see long
tapering log I sit on and barnacles of bark still stuck to
smooth gray grain   in pause of wind (cold wind
constant loud breath   trees' breath)   "winds hold forests
in their paws" (E.D.)   in pause of paws I smell faint almost
acrid sweet of sap glue that sticks bark to trunk   that log I
sit and bask upon in spot of sun came down like a hammer
and ripped apart another tall stump that now stands wrecked
open with its red rust riches tumbling out   and flitches and
flinders of wood

September 24, 2007

      now 38 days   since I looked over gun'l   round
plump gun'l of puffed up inflated launch   down into sea
floor   there below was that great round radiant star Amy
our guide called "sunflower star" with 20 arms creeping over
sea floor over shells & stones & whatever it could seize &
devour   I see also dark misty day   clouds blanking
treetops   and we were out with Amy cruising inlets
beaches   tall grass edges that concealed bears   and
now this   down clear water it oozed along in slow
thorough consumption   this huge "star"

September 27, 2007

      tune   from dream to awake still in me   toodly
woodly widly poo?   no that's loony tunes telephone
I was picking out tune on keyboard   light   bouncy
pop tune I was making up   and H was interfering
interrupting   dedum teedum   teedo   teeda   I hear
it now   tune loony toney tone   tunk tink tan   other
day walking back along creek way I sang "toodly woodly
widly poo"   "   "   "   there's that damned phone
stamp it out stifle it   but what's that all about? I wondered

September 27, 2007

       sky   scald   skill   scold   skel   school
scud   up steep: cobalt toned   gentian   grading
smoothly   sweetly down to powdery blue where white dust
dilutes   down to russet ferns   and I look up   to flash
of sun behind aspen tops glittering and down again to my
monumental stump   great remnant jab of fir whose broken
pieces lie across creek   I see sun catching on threads of
spiders crossing those rising choral lines red gray brown
perfect parallels   upward steps   and other side: myriad
cabinet cubbyholes to hide in   to store things in   beetle
passages

October 1, 2007

       "kiss me once   and kiss me twice   and kiss me
once again   it's been a long   long time"   that tune
slowly ruminatively   played on piano   while on screen
photos of homefront houses in 1944   those notes & chords
stick in me   when I was 14 listening to the Hit Parade on
radio   how to cope with "The War"   how to
comprehend it & all its losses and wreckage   did it have to
be done   gone through   win or lose

October 4, 2007

     Smitty: do you remember   Carolyn Smith
I didn't love you   didn't know what love was   but I
knew beauty when I saw it   and I kissed the prettiest girl
and ran away   that was you Smitty   when all of us
August 1945   were jumping   yelling   screaming in
jubilation   that's how the war ended for us   a moment
of jubilation (as of our team scoring winning touchdown)
and then long life after in which terrible images
nightmares   drifted into us   some of us   one after
another over 60 years   and we who never were in it
could get a glimpse of what they went through

October 4, 2007

at 4 am notes start prancing in my head   licks
and chords   over that steam engine bass   and I almost
tear out of bed and go to the piano to work them out
jubilate   no matter how cold or remote I feel when I sit to
the keys   when I start   sounding   chords   then fire
up the bass   when the whole contraption starts chugging
along   I jubilate   I rejoice   get so charged up I have
to get up & walk out of the room   I love my sounds   it's
different from writing   it's immediate color & resonance
and it all began back in 1944-45   in its way my
answer to all sorrow and misery

October 8, 2007

dear
dire
adore
dour
dower
endure
door

    "adazzle dim"   we saw enormous cloud shadow   a
solid darkness pass   over   Valle Grande   its edges
fine but definite   one side light   other dark   though
the medium was grass   pale yellow ocher   darker   or
brighter as the dividing dichotomy dictated   other shadows
slow flew over that wide plain   after great one passed
sloping plain   dark hills   mountains   surrounding
on all sides   embracing   immaculate shadow

October 22, 2007

       totter   tattered   stutter   titter   tetter   face
and brow tettered with scabs   darts of dermatologist
one big patch high on forehead   ruddy   red   (they
called him "Red" in army)   pale rust strands remnant hair
and he totters   balance lost   so hard to get up on feet let
alone walk   creep   long time   long wait   she holds
on to him   guides steps   stick one side   Joann on
other   they creep   inch along   skin & bones
tattered skin   when he hears you he lights up   and he
speaks strongly   to the point   so bright and humane
so wrecked

October 30, 2007

       overlook above boundary fence
last Friday our walk found leaves still clinging but wind made
them papery rattle   that before even though yellowing
sounded silky suave & light   now harsh crackling sudden
like rattlesnakes
       up here all shorn   thoroughly shorn   pale
greenish gray in masses across valley   now in wind a shorn
sound   forlorn

November 15, 2007

     still see thousands down   not in piles but placed
each and each (on trail ground to meal)   wanwood they
made complete frail cover far & wide   up slope down
slope   (few netted by evergreens Xmas lights)   I came
down once late   in darkening forest trail they spoke and
glowed   amid dark fallen trunks they made a mass of lights
to see by   latest lost   but still traces of yellow in shrivel
so they glowed in darkening woods

December 10, 2007

     Friday   walked arroyo between great bushy piñons
sand river   tracked by last week's rainy night   firm
footing   windy walk   after breakfast in bed   after
where did that come from you wondered   it just came up
(but I knew it came from stroking your hair in the night
the back of your neck up into your hair)

December 20, 2007

      slow across the boards   I walked slow across the
boards   toward the drop   rope around my neck
noose for hanging   maybe it was rehearsal   can't recall
now but step by step   hangman behind me not hooded not
male but a woman   why I was to be hanged?   what
crime   what had I done?   then I fell down to boards (yes
they were wood like flooring) and sobbed and wailed   I
was crying when you woke me   and rescued me from
hanging   I was blowing and gasping   my mouth dry as a
furnace   you pulled me out of it

January 14, 2008

      transit   rapid   tram   train   trong   trang
train   ex traneous   circular train   thanks for the
memory   brain train   caught hold of and runs it round &
round   over & over in my pain pan   Helen woke up one
morning   night full of bad dreams   more and more cars
of sorrow or anger or junk her brain hooked together one after
another   train so long she could no longer pull it   woke
up shaky   felt smaller as if she were growing smaller
miserable   smaller she said growing smaller

January 14, 2008

　　　long　　so long　　stretches out of sight　　it brings
you to a standstill　　stain　　strain　　train　　each
separate car may be paltry by itself　　dismissible　　but all
hooked up together drags you to a halt　　I groped for words
to say to her　　I thought of 'train'　　and that seemed to
help her　　she so receptive　　takes in whatever is offered
in love and sympathy　　and she revives　　miracle of her
resilience　　her vitality wells back up　　amazing

January 24, 2008

　　　words　　just words　　pure words　　goods
woods　　goods　　from the woods　　just words
irksome　　buxom　　just checking out your goods　　here
I like　　see how you flow here　　(yes)　　and this
your grand bowl　　that plumps into me　　(yes)　　when
we sleep　　you sleep　　I awake in "sweet unrest"
sweet undressed　　your great bowl of hips　　rump
plumps into my hollowed stomach　　my arms can cross you
your knees double up so your feet press my knees　　but
these joys must be recorded　　especially when you groan
and stretch tight as a bow against me

January 31, 2008

      fitfully   soft   gently   desultorily   least
breath   it dodges to one side   or   and curls upward?
before waywardly   fitfully   descending   crazy stair
of its own interrupted path   down but in its own sweet time
no push no slant   no drop   but downily   desultorily
downward   switchbacks of no particular aim or direction
but downward in its downy descent   remember a whole air
near and far filled with fitful flakes

February 7, 2008

      petals   clustered hovered over me   clusters
flutter gentle   clutter under foot   dusky   musky
mauve-pink   crabapple   all out overnight   their dark
masses fresh   faint damp perfume   how I adored them
flighty spring   so soon past   I stayed under their thick
dark leaves   dark pinks and mauves   masses   packs
bundles   dwindle   soon gone   dropped   settled
petals   swarmed ground   trampled   blown
shriveled   bits of paper   tissue paper

April 7, 2008

      go chop   slice   cook   serrated knife to slice
red yellow orange pepper chunks lengthwise then crosswise
small colored bits   brown sausage peeled of casing   put
in big black skillet that rings at a tap   spatula it   chop
chop into bits   remove to plate   sauté cipolle   aglio
put back sausage   mix   stir   tap tap clang   steam
rising   add red yellow orange mix   push   scrape
spatula or big spoon   spoony great spoon   pull   push
mix   add hot chile flakes   add red vino   mix   stir
push   push   spoon & spat

April 14, 2008

      gleam   glow of white sails   a fleet rocking north
to south   our 4 eyes embraced   possessed the sight
our backs to fallen trunk   our eyes eastward   how could
our eyes give such godlike embrace   but here in this cool
chilly   almost bitter clean clarity   we saw them
we took them in   we sucked our breath to breathe them in
from base to crown   from dry stony bleak up to snowy
rippling peaks   all their mass being nibbled   gnawed
by patient crawling river

April 14, 2008

     rhymes   always I'm rhyme addicted   always
rubbing one word against another   perfect rhymes are only
the beginning   even better are   reams   rooms
roams   half or ¼ rhyme   alliterating   glitterating
"numerous as space"   numerous   murmurous
numinous   luminous   "a music numerous as space but
neighboring as noon"   etc   etch   it's   bits
slats   sluts   so I came to my streams of rhymes
which looked at one way: 1 word per line – or another way: 1
long vertical line   (almost 30 years ago now)

April 21, 2008

     disjunct   disjointed   scrap of previous   lost
we   you and I   were going down slope through trees to
point of land at lake's edge   a boat was roped to shore
so wind or waves couldn't pull it away   skiff or rowboat
tied with rope   so it would always be there in time of need
sloped woods led back up to houses   and back into lost
dream

May 8, 2008

     long-jawed log sawed in two   gateway path through
deadfalls   so thick in one place   land clogged with dead
long poles over-under-over   land wet   air wet   cold
to breathe   grasses   weeds   occasional trash
kleenex white wad now revealed   bequeathed by retreating
snow   that pounced on it   kept it   hugged it close all
winter   now is giving it back   air cool   cold
shadowed by clouds

May 21, 2008

     even smoother than we really were   all dots
spots blemishes retouched   vague likenesses   myself
homely   spectacled   big-eared   Kennedy droop-eyed
dark full lips   and the snapshots   posed pranks
so poor blurred dim almost fading out of sight   I looked at
1948 yearbook with 60 years between us   it looked
impossible   these were we at our teens   impossible
improbable anyway   because just there I saw us as we are
now   hobbling   Kinney barely mobile on a steel stick
Alex inching along   our hair mostly white or gray or gone

May 23, 2008

     silly lilies   lily sillies   short haircuts   long
wavy tops   Wildroot Creamoil coifs   minimally
recognizable shapes of head   face   chin   round or
square or long   I know them better in little 3rd form photo
42 jammed together on steps (boardwalk in front with snow)
15 year olds   I know each one as I know my own knuckles
& fingernails   there each is   each self   with his hair
shoulders   mouth   and each voice comes to sound
and degree of moustache or beard

May 27, 2008

     pious gloom   gloomy pious   sigh-ous   Ave
Maria in my head   ineradicable   only time will erase
reverent mush (acc. by organ bass pedal notes) throbbing
mezzo   yesterday by Tesuque creek drowned out inner
hum & throb of Schubert's mush   low tympani falls
subtle timbale   water tumbled   creating carpet of white
foam   erupting   submarine gouts erupting   I sat &
my ears & eyes fed and drank full rush of water   May melt
thronging sound

June 2, 2008

　　　　there:
　　　　sound like ship's bow waves constantly thrashing
but forever staying　　　holding (with various shifts &
tremors)　　　as with all this dark water that forms a scape of
hills and grooves　　　gleaming　　　muscular big ripples
and they stay　　　they stay eternal though they're in flow
and their bubbles upwell　　　stream upward to pop　　　eternal
bounty of bubbles　　　gleaming　　　think　　　look: newborn
aspen across meadow　　　new buttery greens shivering
snowflakes dancing　　　bubbles shimmering

June 22, 2008

　　　　leaning dead　　　stronger wind pushes　　　sets up
knocking & rattling in upper reaches　　　"far in the pillared
dark / thrush music went"　　　not pillars like beeches or oaks
tall slim wands slowly gravely swaying　　　while against that
slow rhythm foliage trembles　　　shivers　　　the dead they
uphold leaning long bows against them　　　parallel rush &
tumble of water　　　brought close then away by trail　　　amid
all this　　　thrush music goes　　　child calling into night
but dog will not come

June 27, 2008

dream when I went back to sleep as dawn broke   I
had a plant   a pot I was to take to someone   I went in
room but it was not where I thought   I left pot anyway and
as I went out I encountered woman who lived there   she
would take me where I sought   tall as I   robust smiling
nice-looking   she immediately took to me   put her arm
around me   touched me   as we went along   she led
me down pile of rubble   slipping   sliding   and ruins
of city like Baltimore came into view   tall brick 1940-
vintage apt. bldgs.   but they had holes in them
dilapidated   crumbling   ruined city the smiling
affectionate woman led me toward

July 3, 2008

V. Woolf on T.S. Eliot   "a very self-centered, self-
torturing, self-examining man"   most writers   poets
novelists   Alice Munro   are more or less like that
but some   a few   are hummingbirds like V.W.   their
outward push equal to their inward pull   and how'd she
write so damn much?   for death: "dot dot dot"   "pop
pop pop" (gunfire overhead)   punctuating punch   .   :
;   -   &   ,   peppered with stops& variations of
stops   her diary (expansion of her published writing)
supreme in curtness   her rhythm measured by punches
punctures   I reflect on mine with no punctuation   just
spaces   and it seems very loose & flabby

July 11, 2008

     let me go back into that picture as I would on 2nd
approach to a pastel:
piled up over Lake Peak (just east) and thundering   dark
live   sluggish airy thing with creeping pace south by
degrees   like a starfish (20-armed sea star)   dallying
swelling   cold as winter   I ate at edge of brink of
shadow   where sun hot and cloud cold played to & fro
over me who felt bare legs cold and hot suddenly   and
those clouds that sailed into its maw   changed from
brilliant white to pale icy gray specters   to silverpoint
drawings on dark paper   Durer   agony of Christ   son
in torment   mother fainting

July 25, 2008

     at 24   would there be Silvana Mangano at the end
of the rainbow in Rome?   it was cold   I tramped streets
miles & miles in light raincoat   hands stuffed in pockets
November-December   everyone bundled up but I hadn't
thought   cold caught me in a flimsy raincoat   I tracked
down one monument   then another   back in my room
by Spanish Steps I wrote passages of story or stories   there
was no Silvana 'for me   none to be found   Martarella
was kind but not attractive   Rome not "Roman Holiday"

July 31, 2008

       revolving in our bed we embrace back to front
front to back   feet to feet   hands all over   and I think:
my only true worth and wealth is how I love you   and how
you love me   all else trails behind the love I give you
which perhaps make me worthy of the love you give me
       at 24 I decided to be a writer without much of anything
to write about   and after all the writings since   I see
nothing comes up to our love   except insofar as my writing
is able to celebrate and to love

August 14, 2008

       dream
       not new & shiny   old and stained   blade of
kitchen knife I carried   held in hand   as I left group of
old wandering people   and looked for   what?   no
special goal   but I was searching   out of neighborhoods
into larger downtown bldgs   square led into square grander
and grander   finally a great white church of white stone
grimy   medieval-style   I went toward it holding big old
knife
       and scraps of GI talk   "at ease disease"   "smoke 'em
if you got 'em"   "it'll be your ass"   "never happen,
GI"   "you don't know, do you"   "shit on a shingle"
"I don't know but I believe   I'll be home by
Christmas Eve"

August 20, 2008

"got it made in the shade"   remember we were
draftees not R.A.s   "nickel-assed ree-cruits"   remember
I was pliable then as never since   now not at all   I
submitted & submerged my mind   my desires & needs
tried to be a "good" soldier   remember General Orders we
had to memorize   when guards we stood ranked to be
quizzed by officer   stepped up to each: what is your third
general order?   Sir my third g.o. etc etc   who is your
training officer?   Sir my t.o. is Lt. Kluck   still see him
officious chickenshit 2nd John with his tense grim mouth
his look of command

August 20, 2008

he wore his green cap perfectly stiff blocked with its
gold bar gleaming   he wore glasses   had a beaky nose
acted as if he practiced his look in mirror   to assert
dominance over NCOs as well as us   "good" soldier could
recite Orders   knew serial no. of his M-1   kept in step
and line   rank & file   good soldat did not fuck up &
get in trouble   we complied   penalties were heavy
really silly Goddamn place the US Army   you could take
it only if you turned self into dough to be rolled & punched
into shape

September 1, 2008

     hurry up and wait   as we debarked at Yokohama
we could see head of column down below on land   inched
forward a few feet (up dufflebag down dufflebag)   and all
that long long worm would follow   segments at a time
gradually the shove would work its way back to us   head
of line   checked by NCO who read off names   then
aboard train   night by then   train to Tokyo & repl.
camp   remember large blond GI   NY accent
yelling at Japs standing in stations   "Sakahachi!"   first
Jap words he learned   "suck a cock" it seemed to mean
and he shouted at people staring   and he roared with
laughter

September 8, 2008

     each of these scrawls   a kind of cloud   that after
5 minutes drifts off into nothing   (not a wrack behind)
or shreds   changes   joins another   or a small
iceberg that gradually melts   sucked by ocean
disappears never to be seen again   except writing can last
maybe endure   longer than cloud or ice

September 11, 2008

      up   yonder   when I was up along boundary
fence   came to an easy broken-down crossover   went
down into meadow   found many many gentians   more
than ever I've seen   all warmed   opened by sun
which was now dubious behind clouds (when I came back
later all were shut)   such clusters   lustrous beakers
bees burrowing in   deep blues   blooms   points
6 & 7 buds on one stem   each time I shifted gaze more
came to sight   so many treasures   one stem could
hardly bear weight of so many   drooping   reclining
more & more as I went   deep blues

September 29, 2008

      Riled Rocks   up here at last up here   "the whole
blue fleet in rocking journey state to state"   whole range
of Jemez before me   ending with the tip of Pedernal to
north   walked up through luminous restless yellows
restless masses around me
    big patchy summit below & to west of me (if I were
mountain it would be my left knee) is going from green to
yellow   from yellow to orange   out beyond that
mountain   miles of faint pink low river country

October 14, 2008

    (domiciles)
    spring 1976   this domicile was a brick row house
1914 Pine St. Phila.   converted into 2 apartments   we
had front hall (down to basement were we did laundry)
upstairs along a delicate rickety banister   2nd floor our
living room overlooked street   there in dark I sat looking
at my completed collage created out of Neutral Country
lights of passing cars flowed across that wall   that frame
of color   and made certain glints and gleams of tiny glued
star and bits of plastic for glass   and I was happy being
with it

October 20, 2008

    (New Mexico 1965 – 1975)
    sun pour   sun power   rings of light I see
reflected rings on floor   our white oak floor of wide
planks   sun streamed in tall east window   seemed to
target our grand bed posts   pillars of Karnak   stout
brass columns that rose and flared up into round flat tops
that caught morning sun and put rings of light on floor
our bedroom of our house in Arroyo Hondo   that seemed
to mirror our outer accord   our brass bed like a temple (of
discord)   Chimayó rug   tall curtains   chaise longue
and looking up at rich grooved cedar ceiling between dark
vigas

October 23, 2008

    great house for great arroyo it overlooked following
contour of hill that sloped down toward arroyo with its pale
gray green clumps of chamiso spread over bottom   lowest
(dining) room   looked out big plate glass to west
down deep   wide breach   on up to west & Jemez range
afternoon light that streamed in   blocked & shuttered by
louvers in sala   wind & light pressed against them
 light filtered through slits   wind sounded soft   rippled
louvers

October 27, 2008

     in bedroom   stacked row house   Phila
someone years before us had scratched window pane with
diamond   a date   then "Mrs John Jarvis late
unlamented Jane Jones"   late unlamented   what could
that be I wondered   did Ann gladly submerge her maiden
name (self) in "Mrs Wm Gates"   maybe for a while but
not for long   talk about lamenting   that room and
many others heard her lamentations

October 27, 2008

     arrangements   contexts   rooms   our casa
grande of Arroyo Hondo turned upside down and dumped
forks   knives   chairs   toys   lamps falling
decline and fall of a household   but all planned to fit
somewhere in our next abode (2 yrs) she had everything
placed before we arrived   and everything fit somewhere
brass bed   Sarah's 4-poster   dining table & chairs
nearly all things great and small found a place   a niche
in our 2-year rental   nothing was for long

October 31, 2008

      rewind to 1958 Santa Fe   939½ Acequia Madre
halfway between Acequia & Canyon Rd   2 years married
(I 28 Ann 24) with Sarah 9-10 months   we got 2 rolled
matchstick blinds to cover our bedroom windows   she
made blue curtains for them   I still see that blue   our
bed nothing but mattress & springs on a steel frame   her
tears never seemed they would stop   cry her eyes out like
girl in Struvelpeter   there & thus began our decline & fall
in blue light   swaying wind   matchstick blinds

October 31, 2008

      after 2 years we moved: from 1914 Pine to 1810 Ritt.
Sq.   required down-sizing   some things   brass bed
went back to Santa Fe   some went to Ritt. Sq. condo
which was no home just 2 bedrooms   1 bath   living
kitch-dining   with steel casements and metal rasping
venetian blinds   noisy plumbing next door   & late
night vacuuming above
      & from 939½ Acequia to 512 Camino del Monte Sol
much grander   adobe house   big living rm with hewn
beams   where we put our marital hide-a-bed & other
sticks & hunks of stuff we used in those days   tile table &
old chair we'd refinished

November 1, 2008

what if I'd cried like that?   would it have made any
difference   I don't know   don't forget bench   now
ours here and now in our library   wooden bench
oldest of my old timers   5' long   1' wide on sturdy
angled wood legs pegged up through top
anyway I couldn't   I wouldn't   bench and tile
and round oak dining table   Michael's red bed (one of
twins from Arr. H.) gathered to me   like dear old animals
they comforted me at 601 Sunset St.   and I felt like them
torn away from my roots   pushed & trucked here and
there

November 10, 2008

(Santa Fe 1981)   Helen made me into Will
more and more Bill seemed a poor outworn shell discarded
long ago   late and unlamented   more and more that
remnant-self was of another life   another world   left
far behind   even though I know certain basics lived on in
me   desires   fears   drives   from very early in
life   I now lived with love

November 14, 2008

    keep following traces   trail of things   card table
went with us to Calif.   we threw in our lots together & set
out for   (we still have it wobbly-legged)   it was our
dinner table in Oakland   we sat across card table from
each other   we suffered & tried to tell each other
neighbors' noises   upstairs radio kept blabbing   I
bought a teak desk (still with us)   what else in our meager
ménage?   her bed   her antique dresser   my
Monteith bureau   her down sofas   our commingled
forks   pots   pans

November 17, 2008

    (Seattle 1986)   came home to us her two ancestral
portraits framed in ovals of gilded plaster that flamed out like
sunbursts   these and her beautiful silver   became part
of my life too   as my collage   and my round table
became part of hers   imprinted in our daily usage   and
delight as she imprinted herself   her passion   her feet
her neck   her eyebrows   her contradictory elements
her lust   her strictness   upon my bloodstream and
sinews and mind   truly combined   we triumphed over
our previous lives

December 1, 2008

(Baltimore 1987-1999)
I hear heavy rain outside our windows   daylong
rains   and amid drumming and drips I open small
bathroom casement to hear cardinal chirps "wheat wheat
chew chew chew"   and beyond   faraway   receding
song of train   jazz wail   220 Stony Run Lane   early
spring or late winter dissolving   running away down
gutters   spouts   and outside intimations   light pinks
of cherry across road that glistens wet   sliding under car
wheels   splashing

December 11, 2008

le pourquoi pas pas   the why-not step   such as
sidestep glide Connie Kuhl taught me at Groton dance
Rathbun's girl   went to RISD   cool cat   COOL
slim   aquiline   she knew a thing or 2 or 3   we
danced and   she took hold of me   cheek to cheek
still close   and led me sideways   we sidestepped
le pourquoi pas pas   what I just now name it   why-not
glide   so cool   so sexy   so advanced   she took
me sideways on diagonal through box-steppers & slow
rockers (hands clasped downward   plastered together
2 pillars rocking)   through them   *pourquoi pas pas*

January 8, 2009

came to me early in bed   eyes closed   scene
took shape like dawn in woods as sun gradually filters into
distant trees   then closer like a stage set w. light dawning
memory of September in our first Taos rental   that little
place   I was up early a.m. sitting at crude round leather
Mexican table   I was writing   September cooler and
whisper of rain   wind rustled blind   rain I heard   I
was 58   H& I were in Taos   & our time was coming to
an end   we'd have to return to B'more first of October
whisper of rain became light tapping on roof

January 22, 2009

Mary Elizabeth Moffet Cook?
why not the whole   names resonate (know who it is or
not)   names   sounds   declare human beings
persons   wrap themselves around   inside   outside
persons who say names   and names say them   sort of
"Each mortal thing does one thing and the same   Deals
out that being indoors each one dwells"   so does a name
any name   brunt and forefront of whoever   without
even knowing who
Gaskell   Mortimer   Marlow   Heinsohn   Herzak
Kenworthy   Simeone

February 2, 2009

     (dream)   we thought place was empty   but
then around a corner I saw flicker of garment   into
bathroom I went   and there stood stepmother in bathrobe
she looked invalid   as if terribly sick   her skin white
drained   dark shadows   around eyes   she turned
toward me
     then I was awake   trembling   Helen was pulling
me out of it   soothing   it was nightmare of the undead
I felt skin horripilating up & down my back   why do they
come back   the dead?   because brain keeps them alive in
their lifetime guise   keeps them safe from oblivion
and will bring them forward at certain times   at night

February 5, 2009

       creek   creak   cricket   crack   crooked
creek   first creek in my life - Kishequa   filthy   raw
sewage   wastewater   stringy brown growths flowing
along bottom   but fascinated I was   played in it all day
creek   cricket   first heard then many after dark
even on late cloudy afternoons   night-sound and fireflies
night codes   creek creak of crickets   near & far depth
of sound   (heard it later radio Korea: chirps   cheeps of
Chinese enemy interference) near & far depth of tiny bobbing
lights that we could catch in our hands   green-yellow beams
on and off

February 2, 2009

      such thick mix to word to separate threads entangled:
music from tv "Sense & Sensib."   gentle low notes rising
in patterns on piano then clarinet liquid   longing
soothing   and "hulbert"   then "Hulbert"   my mind
pounces on name and face instantly springs to mind: Korea
then/and (all at once these images)   heavy rain   all day
long pounding down on Monmouth Wales   I'm 18
1948   England   talking in a B&B where I'm staying a
couple days   rain curse of England rain
father paterfam.   proprietor & I talking at supper
his daughters gather around to hear me talk American
"Hants" he says grinning (ants)   and "Alf a crown
'alf a dollar" his grinning face

February 19, 2009

       put   foot   put your arms around me honey
hold me tight   that whore in Seoul   I kissed her   I
think I screwed her   then after out front we sat & I kissed
her   her upper lip curvy & swollen out by prominent
canines   her lips drew me and I really went at her   all
over side to side and inside   roused me again   I heard
soldier watching us he groaned in envy   when we stopped
she said "I like you kissu"   so did I lady   whore
sometime charmer   short-time girl   "cherry girl"
Hendrickson watched us   short burly supply sgt. for 2nd
Sig. Co.   pugnacious   surly   burly   would never
hand over anything without an argument   putcher armsa
rounme honey   hold me tight   (WW II song)

February 26, 2009

      whiteness dream: so-white sun   through light
mist   dispersed light   fuzzy but bright   white boats
small craft   sails all around   lake shore   landing
white under foot of water where boat could push in   you
could wade in shallow over white stone or concrete   wind
winding   mind   wander   windy   window
muttering   wind   wane   wendy   wonder
whiteness of dream boats   lake by city   sails
shallow flat white landing   wading water   wade
wander   wend   window   mutter of wind drumming
glass   drum-head

March 2, 2009

      what did you say?   "mourn?"   piss & moan
enough of that boohoo   laugh   hee hee hee hee
(low) eh eh eh eh   she did what she said last week
came on to me   I mean came onto me   full length
sprawl   pressed me down   naked selves flat pressed
every inch   "boiling" I said "things are boiling now   I
took a pill"   hee hee eh eh   and then she "I feel it
moving"   "Yes"   moving   rising   emerging
and then   spill   bare   joy   bang   bong
dong   prong   ultimate divinity   suffused us

March 19, 2009

      teary eyes blink   & blot to see clearer: drawn:
thrown: brilliant day of lines   white geometrics
tracing blue sky   dark bending bars long across snow
and those dark stripes (each a pride of tree) moved   they
millimeter'd   blinking wet eyes could track their tiny
advance across snow   minutes toward night
omnipotent sun & earth in its flirt or dance with sun
turning   eternal turning diurnal cheeks and faces away but
returning

March 23, 2009

      behind crisscross web of contrails   invisible stars
star stir   stare   steer   sidereal   trades   tried
starry fays   clustered queen moon   tender night
she walks in beauty   cloudless climes   climbing starry
skies   tender   tinder   time to build fire   time to
build & time to give over building   that house took two
years   I see them building   working on walls
parapets

March 26, 2009

    seeding   awake night upon night years back
lifelong   sweet unrest   sweet or sour   baffled
desirous   bitter   sweet unrest   Korea   wakeful
unrest of lust   sleepless   4 hours between guard walks
so much felt   yearned for nightly   and you John if
you'd lived   70   old man like me?   sitting
waiting   hoping for more words?   would your brain
have dried up before   no   immortal bird   never

March 30, 2009

    if I'd known at 25 I was a goner   he knew   but
what great streams poured out of his "teeming brain"
"high piled books" in him to pour out   I   no   not
only no offspring   no wife   no lover   but just what
I had   what I was to those who knew me   at 25 or 20
or 22   like so many who died in Korea   "The Silent
Generation" Life mag. dubbed us   no protest   no
marches no flag-burning   no poetry   no bitter after-
writing   we just went: "came home Friday and went back
to work on Monday" said one

April 9, 2009

      dream   naked   I took all off   stripped bare
I stood among others   Marian Savage alive   she
looked me over   we sat on couch   she looked me up
down in between   her hands stroked my arm   shoulder
she clothed I naked   no sex no lust   just appraising
we never in life   I never but "more nakedly myself" as I
once wrote I wanted to be   that was in Bellevue WA
where I sank low   but dreamy sweater   3 wide bands
of white   beige   cool green   wrapped me when I
rose up
      there to tell you   there in WORDS DIVE   there
to tell you of that glory

May 7, 2009

 lights   dogwood   Vermeer dots
 aurora   salivating
 swarm
light show   Electric Circus   NYC 1969   Ann & I
stood watching   dance of people uncoupled not touching
in flicker & flash of lights   lightning   Electric 2009
Circus   perhaps name for spread of tiny lights swarming
overhead in connecting tunnel to Nat'l Gallery East
people riding roller walkways underneath   many unaware
not even seeing   aurora swarms of lights overhead
constant changing to scatter   stars   dots
        dots white painted wet mouth   liquid of her lips
parted   brilliance outshining red hat   her salivating

May 11, 2009

      we climbed Tesuque Creek in full tumbling goods-
train May melt we climbed   where we stopped   goods
big rocks   water rushing   freight of liquid   liquid
freight   talked   halting   talked   I survived I said
I persisted I said   you triumphed she said   yes I did
paid dear but I
      "Ay in the very temple of delight
Veiled melancholy has her sovran shrine"
by 23   by 24   when I came home via
Snoqualmie I knew what opposite of
ecstasy was   knew well   but I reveled anyway

May 13, 2009

      up Big Tesuque
      this scrumptious creek   parading down its twisted
way   "valley of its saying"   valley of its jubilating
I can't forget this: last year   May '08   I said to the
young woman climbing toward me   "Isn't it gorgeous?"
"Just gorgeous" she said   her voice was full of surprise
and joy
      up here now   creek has taken over path   and
aspens up high are putting out merest tiniest green   my
ears are full of sound of water celebrating   strangers we
were   but for a moment we clicked   we sparked   in
a few words brought close by the water tumbling downward

May 18, 2009

      draw near   draw near again   a sound like distant
parade & band   thumps of drum muffled by distance
draw near   each year we draw near to gulp in that
celebration   in valley of its saying ("poetry survives
in the valley of its saying")   and now the water
ceaselessly generating bubbles like champagne   drink of
celebration   we went up there again to worship   to
wonder   this May melt sounding of many past   life is
the gift (it could be saying)   the only wealth is life

May 28, 2009

       pad   pat   paw   pass   pas de deux
pas-de-deux   pasdedeux   dactylic   tactile
sexual figures flow one to next   nexus   Romeo lifts
Juliet   airborne she turns on him   hangs on him
downward flowing long naked arms   armpits exquisite
around him around and over and under   her buttocks
pressed to him   underarms flow around him pressing their
sleek perfume on him   her crotch   her thighs separate on
him   curves of calves extending   and he
overwhelmed   flooded by her body
actual fucking in & out seems quaint   reproductive
anticlimax   with this ecstasy this climax

June 1, 2009

       spondee   __   __   "stones ring"   "draw
flame"   "soaked rope"   2 slow chords   adagio steps
2 make one Greek foot   but I don't think of foot / feet
 I think of   I count beat not feet   I lay awake silently
sounding & marking Hopkins   long beats "catch fire"
listen: __   __   2 adagio chords   seems simple
enough to scan but it's tricky   not to be pinned down
 one man's spondee is another's trochee   and who's to say
which   who's to pronounce   I say bah

June 4, 2009

        bah   blah   babá   bába   babe   baby
they toted their babies in packs like elephants with howdahs
tottering slightly babes in hats down trail with dog tugging at
leash   but they made it   down steep & across uncertain
logs   across creek without sticks   dog tugging
babies tottering   baby bum   all came back to me
how to change diaper   watching her lift legs slide diaper
under   pins in mouth

June 10, 2009

        dove flutes grave coos   grieving outside my
window   dove mourns   trainsong distant jazz wail
(sounds like trains through Baltimore)   Railrunner sings
cries that special call   I'll find it on piano   and rain
crescendoing   diminuendoing   swelling
diminishing   drumrolling   smothering happy roof
grass   trees   plants   big rain hours long in waves
unlike ocean   or creek steady rush & muffled percussive
bumps   music in my head   new licks   offbeats
Keats   so small a life   but poetry poured out of him
like rain.

June 15, 2009

      not cruel so much as heartless   adventures she
wanted   "time to move on" she would say   turn her back
on lover   husband   connection   and walk
away   perhaps frightened of intimacy   "kindness" he
roared at her "15 years I've been kind"   reminds me of
Karen   Iowa City   she would suddenly slash at me
attack me   I was bewildered   I say now to her "I guess
you do   hate me   you do" when she said   "I could
hate you for being impotent"   she could and did   and
crushed me utterly   how could I salvage myself from that
destruction

June 15, 2009

      at 26 I found love   same year Karen threw me out
how to live on after her   well: protect myself   gird
guard   hide kindness   tenderness   pocket away
build hard shell   cold hard   heatless   but I needed
above all to love someone   so it was futile   no hiding
my need   no pretending to be someone I was not
      rotting they sink   sunk   bones   rags of
moss-covered flesh   rotting forest nurtures bed of bones
merging melting to soil

June 18, 2009

     time   tome   tomb   tombeau   nearby I
noticed big mound   tumulus   ancient fir   red
crumbs   moss   still visible   tree-tomb to be told by
baby conifers rising over it   fed by it   tome of time
in (to decipher) lines   circular pages of grain   hornets
hornets nosed in and out of tor   stump all cracked in
puzzle pieces one side   all rising lines & parapets of gray
grain other side   sheered away to inmost wood

June 25, 2009

     she/he smiles too much   Helen's kids told her that
long ago   most men's natural lip set is not smiling   but
glum or severe   most women's set is smile   not only
but grin   toothy   but that's how we both grew up and
learned in our school yards   to smile or not to smile   to
ingratiate / ease encounters   or to defy / challenge / ward
off unwanted   then I think of tooth care (so American)
every a.m. without fail   time for tooth twine   take little
tooth twine compact   draw floss out to about a foot (more)
snap off   twine around middle fingers   and pluck

July 2, 2009

       child I fastened on mouths   fascinated by lips'
shape   size   color   some curvy   charming
others thin slits   Mr. MacMahon our hist. teacher
"Mr. Mac" had small slit in grim face   bones prominent
big cheek bones over hollow sucked-in cheeks   high
forehead   thin dark hair combed back   and his quiet
(hardly ever raised) voice & emphatic speech   he handed
out memorize sheets (purple mimeograph)   Italian &
German cities that were targets of Allied bombers   we
must memorize   remember "Chee-veeta-veck-ia" he said
carefully   and we must attend

July 2, 2009

       upmost reach of effort   so tired   I found what I
didn't know I was seeking   springs-fed rock garden
rich profusion of plants   blossoms mostly white but
sparked by a few scarlet licks of paintbrush   dropped pack
& sticks   put myself down on flat sun-drowsing boulder
head drooped   eyes closed   surrounded by balmy
trickling   rustling of little rivulets   feeding fork of
creek   sound so soothing a kind of low twinkling
feeding tinkling of small waters

July 6, 2009

      tricks of sticks   ruffle   riff   tricky sticks
rrrrump tick tick tick   (after beat sticks fly up and strike
each other)   licks of sticks   ruffled   rattled our
sticks on hard pads practice   learn rolls   ruffles
for parade all wore cunt caps   puttees   white pants
all 240 marched through village to cemetery   we led with
drums slung over left hip   tricky to tap while marching
Crowell was good (he beat to my boogie   drummed for
me)   drumming while marching   drum shifted
tricks   licks   of sticks

July 6, 2009

      steady   unfaltering   drums proceed up main
street   riffs   rolls   thump (bass drum)
      we wake together under covers to separate ticks
roof over us   licks increasing   glad so we listen
hold each other close   increasing pace   race of rolling
drumsticks   now so loud regiment of drummers drumming
embrace we wrap each other   so happy   now it's
roaring   constant pounding of waves / rain

July 16, 2009

"like as the waves make toward the pebbled shore"
    grind   grist for them "in sequent toil"   incessant
industrious   to make meal out of rocks   sometimes
lapping soft as cats   sometimes churning   tumbling
stones down to pebbles   down to grains of sand   many
tones of gray   white   white speckled black   brown
jade green   polished we found them gathered in hollows
we harvested them   all glossy none bigger than a lima
bean   we gave a bunch to our friend to delight in   their
smooth   glossy   beany   seedy   feel to
squeeze and palpate   like waves sifting

July 23, 2009

    broke heat   great rain   Tues evening
pranced   kicked up heels inside ourselves   delighted
60 next morning   cool cool   and cold up ski basin
where I climbed up trail   smell of dank wood   dead
aspen mold   saw clouds fill valley below as I climbed
above clouds   hands   colder   colder   meadow
where I fed   hands colder   then clouds came floating
through trees   and I breathed in   cold pure mist vapor
I faced   waited   while it wafted through me   around
me   nostrils wide to seek & suck in wet purity

August 3, 2009

    clouds like shifts of mind   thoughts or moods
modify in a moment   great structures   monuments
gone in seconds   I drove us up   twisting   u-turning
toiling up   and over   and down to Valle Grande
sweep of grass plain far away into bends & coves of dark
encircling mts   we got out of car in wind and clouds
cloud shadows crossed the far grass   Amy: "Ah ..." or
"Agh ..."   for bliss or disgust   noting wild flowers
clouds   landscape   "Agh!"

August 3, 2009

    contours of her moving   waves' swells and valleys
as flowing in melt-swollen creek   my hand draws them
exploring my favorite places   we are joined once again after
long away   over-under-over   joined by our
moving flexible mortise-and-tenon   our deep m & t
our legs weave over-under   to contrive perfect moveable
flexible connection

August 24, 2009

    Yuja Wang controlled swarm   led swarm
mastered and turned it up keyboard   down keyboard
great dangerous swarm of bees   Bach bees   in
menacing swarm   she controlled   I hear those many
notes in patterns in various chromatic possibilities tried and
rushing on   patterns I hear each   echoing my youth at
college   Godfrey's records of Serkin & Busch   Yuja
played swarming notes   I hear in mind   & start to nod
and sway   cadenza   credenza   credence
cadence
    hive
    live
    arrive

September 7, 2009

      words ganging up on me: rain cut short my hike
I trudged along double-hooded (anorak & poncho)   2
hoods drooped despondent   view narrowed to path & my
2 sticks out to ward off soaked grass & plants   I stopped
held once again by great swatch of rot   red rust rot riches
of old deadfall   glowing carmine to burnt sienna and
redder: orange rust rotting fiber into flakes   chips
crumbs   particles   splurge of disintegrating wood in
the rain   which shone on bright green grass & leaves that
were slowly swallowing it up   but making it glow all the
more

September 10, 2009

      summer eve   simmer   8   last of sun
horizon shoots level through western piñons   strikes east
corner our wall   shadows of spruce   juniper
against glowing red-gold wall   H: "magic light is here"
she calls
in my dream of lions amid people   I saw female padding
off along distant ridge   touched by late sun   in magic
light   while male climbed nearby tree   and loomed
forward with jaws wide to devour humans below

October 1, 2009

        when I go through door   screen porch into living
room   I get lost in swirls of memory   speculation
faces   voices   but one image strikes through: the
bronze group   3 runners   in a race neck & neck
silhouetted against wide tall casement looking out to front
lawn   South Park Blvd   and woods beyond
springtime   (home on vac. from school or college)
woods still bare or budding   and those 3 in bronze at full
stretch   legs digging   arms reaching

October 5, 2009

        music   "Siegfried's Rhine Journey" I hear pieces of
Wagnerian tones sounding in Gramme's drawing room
(opposite end from straining bronze sprinters)   stood
massive Capehart in its polished wood cabinet
radio-phonograph with changer on spindle   with tone arm
that lifted   drew away while record slid down angle into
receptacle   & another fed from stack above descended
into play position   tone arm up   swung gently to
correct edge and floated down on circling groove

October 5, 2009

       nearby radio-vic stood glass curio cabinet   and in it
marquetry parrot   Italian mosaic of tight-fitted colored
stones against / within black   a picture about 6x9
staring parrot stared out behind glass I couldn't open or find
key   other curiosities but green & yellow parrot holds my
attention through time   while adults gathered around
Gramme to listen to Sunday broadcasts of opera or to her
albums of operas   adults expected to listen & be quiet
while we kids were shooed upstairs to attic playroom

October 15, 2009

       "Now let's just take off this bird" Aunt Jo said & lifted
red war bonnet off my head and set it down on a chair
she was taking pictures   she had short gray hair cut like a
man's   heavy good-humored features (like her father
Caesar Grasselli)   walked with no grace or daintiness but
clumping side to side   (Great) Aunt Jo Grasselli was
taking pix of Christmas dining rm at Gramme Cashman's (her
sister)   big round table all swathed in white linen
special Xmas centerpiece   silver brilliant on sideboard
large ornate pieces   "Cashmanian silver" my father called
it   as in Carolingian

October 22, 2009

      so were maids restrained   hushed   spoke in
whispers   undertones   hushed maids in black and
white   black dresses   white aprons   instructed not
to be familiar with guests   my Ma told me once Annie
was reprimanded by Gramme   told not to be familiar with
guests   even though hushed they smiled & whispered to
us kids   immigrants and their daughters: Hungarian Flora
& her daughter Helen, Anna Lasky from Austria, Margaret
dark good-looking with gap between front teeth

October 26, 2009

      cold   somewhat contemptuous I felt his look
didn't speak much   sandy hair to gray   thick
overhanging brows sandy-gray   big straight Cashmanian
nose   lips tending to pinch scornful   Uncle "Euge"
(rime – 'huge') Cashman   Eugene accent 1st syl. "You-
gene" was how they all said and still say it   "Youge"
I see him striding through room snapping his fingers
tracking down misbehavior   snapping kids into line
light whip-cracks   long stride   "we were all afraid of
him" Joanie said in our old age

October 26, 2009

    Euge   "Youge"   and Bill his elder alcoholic
brother   on & off wagon   joined AA   (sober when
I met him)   but Youge had to (now active head of family)
had to run around & pick up his bro   drunk in some
faraway bar   "all over Ohio" my Ma said   Euge had to
haul him out of gutters   maybe that duty turned him cold
turned him ruler instead of father   he met my Ma after
long absence   "Hello, Frances" he said in cold even voice
stiff as a rod accepted her embrace   Joanie said Nancy
said "he never loved me" and J banged the table in contempt
as if to say   grow up kiddo   get over it

October 26, 2009

    Mommy   Ma   Frances   Fritz   (Francie in
England)   4th child of that house   her father died
Xmas 1928   & Gramme enforced mourning delay of
wedding of Ma and Father   (married at last April 1929)
Boozie Twenties   Father (Daddy I called him)   made
liquor at home   Ma took to drink   ran off 9 yrs later
("9 years I had to wait" she said)   1938   she hated
R.C. church   "all those black priests" she said when her
mother died   alcoholic like Bill?   maybe   she
started drinking midday

October 2009

     misbegotten houses   so malformed   grotesque
lopsided   or pretentious absurdities   malformed
children   houses with birth defects   harelipped
beggars by road   bloated or starving   legless   one
eyed: these freakish habitations amid such magnificence
of land   uplifts   faraway peaks glistening with snow
bosky watersides over-clouded with such soft golden light
land occupied by louts and fools

November 5, 2009

    listing glisten   rolling inshore solace
their sound   not jingle or dry jitter   but constant soft
whir   waves rolling in   I looked up   sun behind
their quills gleamed   color: I stood where I could compare
near vast trunk pink   distant trunk cinnamon   marvel
to see   red-pink vs. cinnamon   slight shimmy
slight bump of hip   informed their shapes   that leaned
as they rose

November 5, 2009

flip back to Standard Time   blink of an eye:
when I went in to doctor it was still daylight   40 minutes
later I came out and it was dark   I saw immense afterglow
cantaloupe   autumnal   overwhelming twilight   as I
drove through street queer feeling   familiar neighborhood
I'd lived here with Ann & kids in 1963-64   twilight
brought it back   house on Allendale St.   I was 33
Ann 29   Sarah 6   Michael 3   Amy 3 months old
and what were we up to at that moment   5:30 dusk
Nov. 3   1963?

November 9, 2009

"the Teenie Weenies"   a gleam in the eye of silver
gleam   polish   banister   enter door of "telephone
room" (cum "cloak rm")   in cupboard: instructive
children's books   "The Goops"   "Struwelpeter"
"The Brownies"   "Teenie Weenies"   and telephone
with chair   through next door into back hall   back
stairs for servants up to servants' quarters over garage
we ran up back stairs to attic   our playground   while
sounded muffled symphonic boom far below   where
grownups gathered in reverence

November 12, 2009

      aisles   I slowed past aspen slope   slim limbers
opened   stood back a bit to give my eye aisle down
through perspective to sunlit sliver far   as I passed I
stepped slow to catch perspectives enfilading   intersecting
radial gaze   found aisle opening up   my eye sighted
along down agreeable verticals   some in light some in
shadow   permitting eye to lock on distant slimmest sliver
light or dark

November 12, 2009

      so out of confusion of memory & thought a rift
opening   a piece of music sounds clear   something
from somewhere long ago   I play it over & over trying to
locate it   where from?   what?   it echoes in mind
day after   days after   but origin is lost   eventually
fades into tangle & static of inner sounds
      so with these tall slim poles   I pass on   and that
narrow clear aisle to a sliver of light is lost   impossible to
find it again

December 3, 2009

     I still hear backup saxes doing their riff behind singers
dee-oodly-oop   dee-oodly-oop-ha   "step aside partner
it's my day"   they were each and all   my days
God it's gone so fast   like a window shade   rolling
faster   faster   to whack   all rolled up tight   each
minute each second   expands into a year   day
mood   snow   dawn   child at window   Ohio
winter   eating snow   snow down my galoshes
wet & cold ankles

December 21, 2009

     staples!   like a baseball seam stitched round
the top of his skull where they'd operated   he was in
hospital   words for Godfrey: to pull him up out of
oblivion death or I or Peggy have put him in   "God-wad"
they pinned on him at school   Storey & Smith & others
mocked & mimicked his tics   grinning Storey with his big
head & big mouth working "om om om om dit dit dit" dit –
clack of his teeth   he never cleared out those tics   still
doing them in old age

December 24, 2009

      G's mother drove him around Baltimore   loony bin
(Shepherd Pratt)   "Your father is in there," she told him
penned up in there   jailed in there   G never knew his
father   hush-hush in those days   someone cracked up
put him away in asylum   "insane asylum" had a dread
sound to it   shh   4th form year they told him his father
had died   maybe he always felt strange   a stranger
outsider   outré   year older than us   jeered at
mocked for his tics   hushed stories about him   rumors
of dirty doings in basement with so-and-so   he told me
later when we were roommates at college   talking far into
night

December 28, 2009

   "happy and sad   sad and happy" I heard him say
telephone   at college   answer to how was he
(some girl other end)   exuberant at school he and
Crossman sang McNamara's Band again & again   never
seemed to weary of it   asinine   " a credit to old
Ireland"   happy smile as he hollered the words   ups &
downs   a bit manic
   when I saw him again after army he was married and
dull   dulled down   he seemed down   as if life had
gone out of him   selling stocks   "investment analyst"
his wife beat him down

December 31, 2009

       she'd break your balls soon as look at you   G's 1st
wife Jean   ball-stomper   coarse   jeering   harsh
and he'd even dated her at 18 and <u>knew</u>   shock to me
when I (23 in Korea) got their wedding notice   what was
it   why   that bitch   no wonder when I saw him next
he seemed lifeless   flat   she'd flattened him   and
steered him away from religion & divinity school
his bent   into support-type job   stocks & bonds   he
was religious   to go with his excesses of hilarity and
sadness   why Jean?   and he stuck in that misery 15
years

December 31, 2009

     why Sue Ann?   years passed with no word
when G was 43   he and his wife Sue Ann came visit us
she was hefty (he liked 'em big)   red-blonde   mole on
cheek   he'd picked her up in NY dance hall   on return
we stayed overnight with them   he was making big bucks
"six figures" she said   they took all of us to "Godspell"
     when he was 48 he stayed a night in Phila with us
took us out to dinner   and told us Sue Ann was cruising
bars & picking up men   he said "I put down my fork and
almost barfed" when she confessed all this to him   she
was a whore   which he knew she had been when he
picked her up and made her his wife

January 7, 2010

     words for G   we heard him talking on telephone
sotto voce   next room   after midnight   when we
were in bed watching lights slitting through louvers   our
corner condo bedroom   we heard G   soft talking to his
new love   she was married   (she followed Sue Ann)
1978 or 79   so he was near 50   at 50 he was
reconstructing   reconjuring his love life   but it fell
apart   but she bequeathed him Peggy   her friend

January 7, 2010

     Peggy became his new new love   as one
disintegrated   another lifted him up   G was eternally
ready for love   I from my safe box of unhappy marriage
watched him amazed   what was love   how could he
but there's no cutoff point for love as I was soon to find out
she will   could   can   come along and seize you and
lift you straight up high over her head   and bring you
down slowly gazing into you all the while

January 14, 2010

        words for G

        G inching hobbling toward me   my mouth must
have gaped   he started to laugh   brain surgery had
paralyzed his left leg   we'd got tickets for Orioles   to
meet outside ballpark   first I knew of his laming
permanent cripple last ten years of his life   he was 67
lived   struggled   thru ten more   immobile   had
a wreck in car   no more driving   after game I hoisted
him up   all my might   up he came with a laugh
kept a good humor good face as long as he could   but fury
lifelong furies   bitterness   started to erupt against
Groton   against his sisters   remember H & I arriving at
their house to hear his voice roaring in spew of rage   he
was on telephone to sister

        Godfrey gave what he had   he gave love   life
was too much for him   but he took it in good spirit
he lived it willingly   and bravely

January 25, 2010

     5 p.m.   glass door of bedroom   we sat & read
our books   turned to look out through glass   sun
setting caught big icicle   illumined all its brilliant hard ins
& outs   golden light infused ice   wall spotted soft
dapples   O's   red ocher   inside our room touched
mahogany   she says I'm not cold-hearted   may be love
has so infused & warmed me I hardly notice anymore   but
I'm better for it   stronger   happier   more than I can
realize   others feel it in me

February 17, 2010

    what a road   rolling south until no more trees
only low green scrub for miles   always surrounded &
overlooked by up-thrust peaks   bare pinnacles   fortress
of cliffs that rise up slant   like men with chins stuck out
nowhere is it flat nothing   everywhere   spying peaks
far & near   peak to poke   to mountain to butte to jut
to swell   land in motion   restless earth

February 17, 2010

    Tucson: precise pricks protect garden fractious
succulence   up in Cousin Allie's suburb   houses
incorporate cactus   prized & cultivated   prickly pears
in varietal symmetry   various schemes of spines   they
pop out of one another lobe upon lobe   their oval purple
or green flat lobes   incredible structures like houses of
cards   some cacti sprout occasional sparse spines like
hairs on a hand   others radiate spines in cluster and rows
upon huge bulging heads just protruding from earth

March 10, 2010

    time to move pencil   4 am   bed   dark
awake   she's awake   something tickles her   her
deep   lusty   guttural   eh eh eh   such big sound
from her small body   I push out of bed   "Are you
going to the bathroom?" she says in loud voice   other
times her voice in husky sleep asks or tells some fragment
she   and I'm crazy about her again   she's part of me
like an arm or a leg   part of my thought & sense

March 11, 2010

      okay   comic relief   for grim stories   gloomy
plays   why not farts   yes farts   grumble   grouch
gloom   *   (reader must supply noise)   ooh ah sob
sob   *   (reader supply sound)   solemn
longueurs   punctuated by   *   *   *   time to
inject some comic relief   or now and then a belch
(God am I ever belching these days   and farting
constant accompaniment   tympani to my days)   new
and original literary device   (at least since Chaucer)
(also Leopold Bloom on the pot)

March 15, 2010

      sky above her   reaching long white filaments
mares' tails   cirrus sweeping   as she lay back on her
backpack   to soak in sun and sky   her glasses turned
dark   geese we heard warbling high above   and at last
saw in their wavering Vs   several echelons   one
behind another   she soaks   absorbs   these things
and they give her joy   she recalls before sleep her favorite
moment   other night after unwelcome phone call her
mouth turned down   down & down   so steep
distress & anger   steep as St. Louis arch

April 1, 2010

      dream this a.m.   I climbed back up   though
party was finished   steep hill   paths & stairs   to say
thanks to Libby   (I was dressed for wrestling   had
booklet   instructions   knew naught of wrestling)
but wrestl. match was postponed   I wore shorts   t-shirt
for wrestle   I came up to Libby with thanks   but
flowers of my speech were   stale   withered   I hope
you can relax now I said   and she looked at me
smiling dubiously as if to say   relax? are you kidding?
now they had all the cleanup to do

April 5, 2010

      serpent in semicircular curve   semicircular ocular
serpent of light   vibrating brights   zigzag pattern of
African snake   gaboon viper   venom of African
vibrant C   shimmering chimera   visits me when I
abstain from aspirin   it grows from a spot   occludes
vision   blocks reading focus   must close eyes as it
grows & grows   takes over left side of left eye
shimmering   dazzling neon   or crescent moon snake
chimera   then gradually drifts off stage left

April 12, 2010

now another staging of Anne Frank   played as
sassy   self-centered   obnoxious   as well as fearful
loving   bright   in 1980 I went around Secret Annex in
Amsterdam   I told H. she rather than Virgin Mary could
be our hope (as H put it) for future   with all her faults
not V.M. not superhuman   but nonetheless our hope our
feminine hope   but would she still when she was dying at
Belsen   would she still say "in spite of everything I still
believe people are good at heart"?   she might not have
<u>but she might have</u>   we'll never know

April 29, 2010

(on great ridge facing southwest high up Chamisa Tr.)
part gray   part glowing yellow   resinous
rub   rub resin   frictious   faint delicious on thumb
this root this flame twisting upward   overturned roots
one piercing upward   flame-curving in & out   sinuous
curves   this treasure   how many have never   will
never see   I've found and marveled   when roots rip up
out of earth they bring stones in their grasp   but this long
how long   hundreds of years?   is that what they tell
and this one flame   weathered   burned   scourged
down to pure heartwood

April 30, 2010

       dream   3 am   heart-rending dream   party
somewhere   and a band   3 trumpets   3 great
players   3 sharp silvery horns in harmony
"Moonglow"   those chords rang out   to dance!   I
saw you   I had to dance to Moonglow   you saw me
and always ready to open your arms to me   and dance
you came toward me   my one & only all-out lover
       and then I was awake   torn out of dream   or did
I abandon my happiness   did a sound wake me   a
crack in a joist   ache of loss   but you and music are
not lost   they are there   always ready   you lose me
in dreams   but I'm ever there   wrapped around you.

May 17, 2010

       dark green   or hazel   her eyes large   staring
at me   woozy   drowsy   coming to after surgery
her eyes stayed on me   in small room   too small for 2
yet another was there   look away as I might   or around
or at something else   her eyes stayed on me   her voice
slow & rasping & hoarse   3 hours they said & 3 it was
they 2 talked to J & me   all was well   her insides
looked fine   I kissed surgeon's hand

May 20, 2010

     above: theater of ethereal   silent   moving
west to east   clouds   being shredded   being
shreds of being in the making   tatters groping
writhing for form or nothing   clouds being bundled into
enormous shapes   below: creek roaring full of snow-
melt torrenting   overriding all other sound   confined to
shape of its carving   for all its foaming rush set in a shape
of motion

May 24, 2010

     at 16 I wrote his name on blackboard with chalk
I wrote name of my love   and lust   in classroom
after hours I wrote it   because I was impelled to write it in
empty classroom despite my secrecy my fiercest concealment
and G looked in   saw it   said his name in kind of glee:
aha – caught you!   smell   or sound   or some
emanation told on me all along   never so locked up inside
never so secret as I thought   I gave myself away in spite
of myself

May 27, 2010

      I climbed upstream   took pictures of grand aspen
deadfall   one over another   over & under & over
grand pickup-sticks jumble   and of blooming foam in
swollen creek   when water plunges into pool   churns
up big blossom of foam   continuous shifting   tumbling
blossom   exfoliating   changing   staying   I feel
sexual   that bubbling blossom must be like her when she
comes   she says it reaches all her extremities   I
remember times we've had   coming together   huge
blossom forming   vanishing   forming again   within
her where I'm plunging

June 3, 2010

       alive alive-oh   while I'm alive   man alive
aspen leaves along stony road I climbed   just out full
a little higher just born   shiny   waxy from womb
further up   sweep of green mist   leafies just pushing
out   further still gray   smoky   and I 80 trudging up
stones & dirt   2 sticks tapping   2 young passed me
he bare waist up bare   gleaming young skin & muscle
she short blond hair   both in shorts   passed me in easy
strides   every year it happens   birth of millions of tiny
waxy leaves   I keep hold of physical strength while I live
       inside   my spirit sometimes so old & worn

June 10, 2010

      "take all away from me but leave me Ecstasy"
power & ecstasy within her   "no one swaggers now but
me"   all that bank of words (wild words)   all that
mountain pent up   spring rush   no wonder   but all
wonder   she lived secluded   to bring it all out
she must   required solitude   not secrecy   not
conventual   she must have solitude   no less to work
out that power   tap it out (I can see her fingers tapping out
her beats)   "the bobolink is gone   the rowdy of the
meadow   and no one swaggers now but me"

June 17, 2010

        sea quotes forest   wind strokes both   agitated
quiet   still sensitive   high silken sound   draw
sapling to you   hear its rustle of silk   high strung
even quiet one leaf twirls   up high tall stalks largo
swaying metronomes   masses of light   masses of dark
interpercolate   swinging   roaring in breath across them
then still   but not quite quiet   shadows of leaf on leaf
leaf dark green in shadow   yellow green in light
sea-shuffle of sparkle   darkle

July 8, 2010

        magenta   I hark back to our time in Seattle
because that's where began all these quick takes   flash
writings   fleet notes   that zero in on "the present
palpable intimate"   present in past   past vital in
present words   Mt Ranier   its magenta paintbrush
tall forests   remnants of origins   hemlock   cedar
spiking up 200 feet   green spiky devil's club   deadfalls
smothered in moss   on up   on & on & up   to
Melakwa Lake quivering green & blue   there & then I
began to fly   with these quick takes

July 12, 2010

      admire: I watched her pushing up ahead of me
her legs study from her dedicated morning walks   never a
falter   now & then a sip of water a breather   strong on
her feet as I   she climbed steeps & toughs up from valley
10,400 up 300 – 400 feet to Wilderness Gate   admire!
And it didn't exhaust her   and it made her so happy
hearing thrushes calling   feeling cool in aspen flutter
just being there   so happy & pleased

August 30, 2010

      blue horns unfurl   renew each morning   not
toward sun   but all after departing night   new blue
trumpets   soundless chorus   4's   5's   glories
petals like finest thinnest skin   unfurled and gaping wide
yesterday's already shriveled   today's clamoring
blues each marked with long-pointed narrow white star of 5
prongs   silent anthem   not for sun   but for last
night   for disappearing stars

September 8, 2010

      dream   I was with cousin Joan Cashman   she
told me she'd run away from home when she was a child
then I was with her parents   talking to Aunt Peter (she
looked fine   pretty   as she did when younger)   I
was asking her about things   what she thought   she
said "I think about the future"   I told her what J had said
abt. running away and P said "Oh – yeah – "   as if
bringing memory back from long lost

September 20, 2010

      all signs agreed   planets in conjunction   stars in
line   internal organs at peace   omens favoring
nakedly we   she lowered herself on top of me
unrolled herself like carpet   legs   hips   belly
breasts   first in long long time   I felt delight of groins
combining   pressing   sly crinkly embrace of V's
so we rippled   I lifted   rose   and fell   our pubic
joint juncture   moved as waves while rest was still   my
hand free to roam back of her neck   such a charming

September 22, 2010

      dream cities   dilapidated   grimy   dingy
streets   nondescript seedy bldgs   this one no different
but I had companion   Steffi   Swedish   dark pretty
young woman   we sought train   to ?   she found it
by long line of people waiting   Steffi knew it was right
line   she ran with quick steps to get in line   I lost her
line longest I ever was in   station was wrecked as if
bombed   I felt her 2 arms come around me from behind
I found her!   Steffi

September 30, 2010

      fierce rushing   "here - here - here
- here -" they cried   wings whickering they
alighted in piñons   grabbing gleaning nuts   faint
crackling as they jabbed for one last nut   (late they came
cones already open   most nuts dropped)   piñons shook
& tossed under their attack   they searched &   poked
hung upside down on bobbing twigs   lost hold
dropped   caught selves   and raced away   pulling
one after another after them   until all flocked away
"here"   "here"   to another grove   into sunlight that
blued them   jays

October 7, 2010

      no dream this: edge of a Gatsby-like party
night   stars if not moon   the girl sat on a chaise longue
I at her feet or beside   and we almost fell in love
found sympathies   affinities   many links of thought
feeling   how did she look in the luminous dark   (I'd
just met her)   dark hair in a bob   tall   with full red
lips   nearby sounds of dance under a great tent   we
found each other in 1952   it seemed we had a glowing
future   but very soon not   we crashed   what
happened?

October 7, 2010

we went on a picnic   just we two   cruel
crippling silence fell over us   all talk vanished   heavier
it got the more locked up we were   had we exhausted all
talk?   no   but   did she feel it was all too fast & she
grew afraid?   no knowing   we never talked again
she never said what ate at her   nor did I   our final
encounter was bitter   at her door   -   she opened &
saw me & frowned   -   she turned silently   walked
off through house   disappeared   left me at door   as
if I were last person she wanted to see   I was drafted in
August   never saw her again   thankfully   but
regretfully   lasting regret

October 14, 2010

Michael: mesas   -   "flat-top haircuts"
their level tops   that drop off short & sharp at ends   I
see his benign amused smile   his thickly dark-stubbled
cheeks & chin   his long dark hair   flowing back over
his head & neck   he seems so easy & benevolent   yet
so intent when focused on our electronics   fixing our tv
sound   connecting speakers   Michael at 50   Helen
says he's a honey   loves Trollope   & classic things
also Harry Potter & fantasies

136

October 18, 2010

      nearby we delight in a leaf just landed   from afar
we our eyes fan wide over valley full of pastel strokes and
soft merging yellow to red to orange to russet to lilac gray
all flowing   glowing across watershed   and on up
slopes of enormous bald mountain opposite
      with soft query gray jay alights   until we toss bits
of nut   more fly in   wings wuther   flutter   pale
gray with black beaks & eyes   so sharp their eyes   to
find & nip up bits no matter how obscure   one brushes my
hat flying in
      our nearby amusement   to pull eyes from
faraway wonderment

October 21, 2010

	dell	stell	cell	del icate	knell	
dwell	fell	still	skill	till	gill	grill
nil	nell	bell	will	well	wall	will
wile	Nile	stile	tile	file	fill	fell
full	bill	chill	dill	dell	grill	jell
kill	lil y	mill	pill	pull	quell	quill
rill	still	spill	shell	tell	yell	spell

November 1, 2010

      drink bells   clink time   trink time   tinkle
ting-a-ling   go glasses   ice   watch the tray
approach   icy glasses   icy sounds   yellow curl of
lemon   first sips: ah that is so keen   so chill
passing down palate after tonguing around mouth   drinks
à nous deux   my parents had a little glass shaker that said
"à nous deux" written on it   now we gather together after
a long day   we salute each other

November 8, 2010

      some moments   certain amount of mome raths
outgrabe   I looked for rhyme for 'wave'   as usual
ticked off alphabetical 'aves'   came to 'r'   rave
nave   crave   etc   rave?   raven!   it struck me
there it was   not just my rhyme but entire lift-off from
two humans at brink of mesa   now two ravens   black
birds riding updraft along brim of mesa   riding wave
whole poem picture transformed   in one stroke

November 22, 2010

     why   ignorant   indifferent   so many of us
some can't   some too busy   some don't care   why
many here care a lot   Nature is so close   but even here
people we know don't care   don't connect   how can
they not embrace what is our greatest treasure   next to life
itself   Nature   life and death of trees   I found a
good quiet sunny spot above trail   in embrace   in nest
of fallen ponderosa

December 2, 2010

     early   early nightfall   sun sinks at 430   light
orange mellow cantaloupe   I watch apparitions on wall
blinds' parallels   chest   color phantasms   broken
rectangles softly outlined   limned softly   such rich
projections   afterglow   at 630   7   engulfs
horizon   spreads upward   fades into night blue   sun
sunk   then "night   that seals up all in rest"   and we
try to stay warm   coldest November we ever knew

www.ingramcontent.com/pod-product-compliance
Lightning Source LLC
Chambersburg PA
CBHW022010080426
42733CB00007B/553